PRAISE FOR *LEAD TRUE*

"Thompson is a practical visionary. He not only envisioned a broader healing mission for healthcare that encompassed his community and the planet but also created a powerful example of this vision through Gundersen Health that has become a beacon of hope for the country and the world."

—**Gary Cohen,** President,
Health Care Without Harm and Practice Greenhealth

"This is an incredibly important book; it goes to the heart of achieving truly successful leadership. It is not about technique, manipulation, or cutthroat management; it is about combining competence in leadership with principled leadership that recognizes that helping others be successful is the responsibility of a true leader. Jeff uses real-life examples that illustrate the challenge of not only knowing what is the right thing to do but having the courage to do it. Demanding excellence from ourselves and others in a fair and just way may often be challenging but ultimately is essential to meeting our responsibilities and achieving real success. The examples he uses will spur wonderful and fruitful discussions especially in young leaders."

—**Sister Carol Keehan**, DC, President/CEO,
Catholic Health Association

"We can lead from any seat in the organization as this wise, beautifully written book makes abundantly clear. *Lead True* gives a wonderfully authentic look into what it takes to lead a journey to excellence."

—Leonard Berry, Ph.D.,
University Distinguished Professor of Marketing, Mays Business School, Texas A&M University; and Senior Fellow, Institute for Healthcare Improvement

"*Lead True* will make you a better leader. If you are already leading, this is a must-read. If you are new to leadership, this is the definitive guide. Thompson's value-based leadership journey will take you on a magic carpet ride. Following Thompson's principled lessons, you will develop your leadership, your organization and its people will improve, and your community will flourish."

—David T. Feinberg, MD, CEO,
Geisinger Health System

"Jeff Thompson has captured the essence of what excellence in leadership looks like. The riveting true stories in this book inspire and challenge us to reexamine our own core beliefs."

—John Toussaint, CEO, Catalysis,
author of *On the Mend*

"Jeff has been an advocate of doing the right things the right way for many years. As a health and business leader, he has led the way on responsibility and sustainability. I appreciate his insights and am challenged by his approach to put them in action."

—Walt Rosebrough, CEO, Steris Corporation

"Healthcare remains the number-one economic and social issue of our time. As such, it's an industry crying out for principled leadership based on strong vision, mission, and values. *Lead True* is a must-read for anyone trying to marry business principles for strong organizational leadership with an obligation to deliver a societal good."

—**Susan D. DeVore**, President and CEO, Premier, Inc.

"It's one thing to write about values-based leadership. It's altogether another to live it. In Jeff Thompson's case, he has now done both in a truly thoughtful and inspiring way."

—**Laura A. Jana**, MD, Author, *The Toddler Brain: Nurture the Skills Today that Will Shape Your Child's Tomorrow*; Director of Innovation, UNMC College of Public Health

"This book is inspiring, helpful, and important. The lessons and stories put you in the shoes of leaders facing the very challenges we all see in healthcare today and provide practical ways to look at leading. Every student of healthcare leadership can learn from this book, and even more importantly, every leadership team from healthcare organizations and systems today can use the lessons from this book to build strong and moral principles for leading to the Triple Aim of better health for our populations, improved healthcare, and lower per capita costs for our communities."

—**Maureen Bisognano,** President Emerita and Senior Fellow, Institute for Healthcare Improvement

"The most important thing to know about Jeff Thompson is that he is for real; he lives and breathes the courageous, compassionate, values-based leadership of which he writes. It's no wonder that he led Gundersen Health to embody authentically patient-centered care—and his insight in how leaders can build healthy organizations and communities is a must-read for anyone seeking to effect meaningful change."

—**Rebecca Onie,** cofounder and CEO, Health Leads

LEAD
TRUE

LEAD

TRUE

LIVE YOUR VALUES,
BUILD YOUR PEOPLE,
INSPIRE YOUR
COMMUNITY

JEFF THOMPSON, MD

ForbesBooks

Published by ForbesBooks, Charleston, South Carolina.
Member of Advantage Media Group.

ForbesBooks is a registered trademark, and the ForbesBooks colophon is a trademark of Forbes Media, LLC.

Printed in the United States of America.

10 9 8 7 6 5 4 3 2 1

ISBN: 978-1-946633-01-9
LCCN: 2017936553

Cover design by Katie Biondo.
Layout design by Megan Elger.

This publication is designed to provide accurate and authoritative information in regard to the subject matter covered. It is sold with the understanding that the publisher is not engaged in rendering legal, accounting, or other professional services. If legal advice or other expert assistance is required, the services of a competent professional person should be sought.

Advantage Media Group is proud to be a part of the Tree Neutral® program. Tree Neutral offsets the number of trees consumed in the production and printing of this book by taking proactive steps such as planting trees in direct proportion to the number of trees used to print books. To learn more about Tree Neutral, please visit **www.treeneutral.com.**

Since 1917, the Forbes mission has remained constant. Global Champions of Entrepreneurial Capitalism. ForbesBooks exists to further that aim by bringing the Stories, Passion, and Knowledge of top thought leaders to the forefront. ForbesBooks brings you The Best in Business. To be considered for publication, please visit **www.forbesbooks.com.**

*This book is dedicated to all those who have the courage
to live their values in the public crucibles of struggle
as well as in the quiet where no one might see.*

TABLE OF CONTENTS

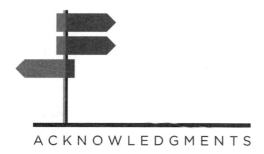

ACKNOWLEDGMENTS

Gratitude seems far too mild. Without the guidance and contributions of others, this work would have struggled, like any of us without air or water. Without them, I and this work would not exist.

I'd like to thank all the educators, pastors, scout leaders, and family who helped me transition from a ragged little kid into a student with a purpose and a desire to serve. And I want to recognize Dwight Klaasen, Jerry Strohm, and William Spofford at UW Platteville who trimmed my overconfident edges, taught me to learn not memorize, and pushed me past my occasional mediocre effort. Thank you.

Liz Silverman dominated my medical school time with loving haranguing and demanding pressure. She pushed and pushed but deeply supported. At my residency, we had national icons but the bedside was learned at the broad shoulders of Dave Clark: smart and caring, practical and intensely knowledgeable, always contributing far above his recognition level. Post training, Don Berwick and Maureen Bisognano have done the most to improve care, lower costs, and teach me and us about our broadest responsibilities. They stretched me; Lee and Leanne Kaiser expanded me. Thank you.

To Kari and Becky, thank you.

At the center of our accomplishments at Gundersen are the hearts and work ethic of thousands who led, worked, cared, and breathed the values in the face of hardship, pressure, and a less-than-perfect work environment. The contribution of those staff in concert with our community partners to the health and well-being of the region cannot be overestimated. Such passion to serve, whether in the spotlight or in the quiet of the night. Thank you.

The contributors you will meet have shared their most personal stories in a way that will help you lead groups of two or twenty thousand. It was so gracious of Mr. Immelt to share his insights when I am well aware he has many other very important pressures. Thank you.

To the many staff members at Advantage Media Group who have helped move this project from a gaggle of ideas to a useful collection of stories and insights to help others serve the greater good. Thank you.

And finally, and most importantly, to Sandy who had the courage to marry me, the perseverance to stay with me, and the durability to be the best model of a values-led life. Thank you.

LEADERSHIP MATTERS: THE TIME IS NOW

Jeffrey R. Immelt, Chairman and CEO, GE

Jeff Thompson has led one of Wisconsin's largest health systems through significant growth, innovation, and change over the past two decades. He sometimes describes himself as "an old ICU guy who lives in a farmhouse," which shows his genuine modesty. An accomplished physician, leader, and businessman, he cares deeply about making life better for people.

Jeff has devoted his career at Gundersen to the organization's mission, improving the health and well-being of patients, families, and communities. As he rose to positions of leadership, Jeff supported the Gundersen mission by investing in talent development and creating a structural basis for innovation. Even through economic downturns,

Jeff and Gundersen continued to invest. Today, Gundersen Health System has achieved considerable success through high-quality patient care—and through a focus on leadership and culture.

Leaders must be clear about what they believe in. Your beliefs provide the foundation that helps you stay resolute and resilient. Yes, change requires adaptability, but you must balance that with a core vision and viewpoint that will allow you to achieve results over the long run.

When Jeff asked me if I would be willing to contribute a few thoughts to a book he was writing on values-based leadership, I was eager to do it. Leadership and healthcare are two of the most important issues of our time. They are certainly important to me. Before my current role, I ran our healthcare business, which was then called GE Medical Systems. Gundersen was one of GE's customers, as they are today. They have great people and are committed to serve. I am proud to work with them. I am invested in their success.

If you look at our respective organizations on paper, we look different. However, we are in fact very similar. On paper, Gundersen is a nonprofit, physician-led organization of about seven thousand employees, a regional innovator that has earned national recognition for patient care. GE is a digital industrial company that employs more than three hundred thousand people worldwide; about one-sixth of them work in GE Healthcare. We operate in 180 countries. And we invest more than $1 billion per year in research and development for our healthcare business alone.

At our core, both organizations—Gundersen and GE Health-care—are keenly interested in advancing every phase of patient care. We want to improve healthcare productivity, affordability, and quality to improve patient access and outcomes.

We also believe that culture is a platform for transformation and growth. Build a culture that honors the passions and aspirations of your people, and you stand a much better chance of meeting your mission.

Jeff has done an outstanding job of this across Gundersen. As a result, the organization is among the top 1 percent of health systems in the United States.

The team at GE Healthcare has intensified its focus on culture over the past year as well. The organization's new purpose statement, "Improving lives in moments that matter," reflects the team's passion, commitment, and competitive drive. I am excited about the progress they are making. It is something the rest of our company will learn from.

This is a consequential time in healthcare. The decisions we make today—concerning everything from treatment protocols, to digital strategies, to clinical operations improvements—will affect the global healthcare system for decades. It comes down to leadership.

GE is a proud leadership company. But strong leadership development is emblematic of the best organizations in any field.

The world needs leaders who can take smart risks, adapt to context, make decisions, and see them through—leaders who have a sense of mission; commitment to core values; dedication to community; and the courage, durability, and discipline to persevere.

This book is an investment in those leaders, the cultures they build, and their ultimate and lasting success.

YOUR PERSONAL COMPASS

On summit day 2007, Julio Bird and his team found themselves on the north side of Mount Everest. The team of four Western climbers and three Sherpa had come a long way together, but their journey had not been smooth, thanks to friction between the Westerners. The low-level, ongoing conflict had disrupted the trust that is so critical to optimal team function. As the group became increasingly divided, some members adopted a self-protective, selfish stance and focused on looking out for only themselves.

Teamwork unraveled, and bad things started to happen on the final ascent. One team member, who felt insecure about the others' commitment to his safety, turned around without telling anyone and abandoned the group; even worse, he took with him a Sherpa guide and valuable oxygen bottles. Another insecure member of the team began using oxygen at an alarming rate; he would soon run out and, as a result, needed significant Sherpa support. When Julio's team had reached the obstacle called the Second Step, about eight hundred vertical feet and three hours from the summit, simple arithmetic revealed that the team's oxygen would run out in the next few hours, leaving nothing for the perilous descent.

As the leader of the team, Julio was faced with a critical decision: should they push on, despite the risks, or should they all turn back? Julio was personally eager to reach the summit, a goal he had set himself. He knew, however, that the team was counting on him to make the right decision. If he chose poorly, lives could be lost. He needed to set a course that was led by courage and strong values, one that led to the best possible outcome for everyone concerned.

Julio decided to lead three members of the team back down the mountainside, while the two stronger climbers went on to scale the summit, bringing with them sufficient oxygen supply. This meant that Julio would not achieve his personal goal of reaching Mount Everest's summit. However, his decision assured that two climbers would reach the mountaintop and, more importantly, everyone would return safely.

Julio demonstrated true values-based leadership. His willingness to find a compromise, one that maximized the common good and rose above selfishness and insecurity, ensured that everyone was safe. His discipline and his willingness to set aside his ego protected the lives of those he led.

This is the kind of leadership that sets a course for others, bringing them to a destination they couldn't have reached alone. Leadership like this isn't about the person who leads as much as it is about the values that inform them. Leaders like Julio set the course that ensure the well-being of everyone.

You and I may never scale Mount Everest, and we may never face the life-or-death leadership challenges Julio faced. However, as leaders in the worlds of business, education, or government, we have to face our own moments of crisis. Each of us must decide whether we will follow our ego-centered inclinations, or we will lead for the good of everyone whose lives we touch. Will we endanger or impair those around us to satisfy our own self-interest? Or will we lead in a manner that is true to our values?

Imagine, for example, that you are a newly trained doctor. You are skilled but you have barely begun your career when the ICU nurses ask you to treat a very ill child, despite the fact that a senior doctor has made the decision to postpone treatment. What do you do? If you follow protocol and abide by the other doctor's decision, the child may die. But if you intervene against the doctor's, you could lose the position you have spent the past ten years working to achieve. Which is more important—saving a life or keeping your job?

What if you are the CEO of a company that is barely breaking even and you learn that a competitor is in even worse shape financially, eliminating some of its services as a result. The community's well-being depends on those services, but it will be costly for your organization to take them over. Do you play it safe and allow the community to suffer, or do you take on the challenge of providing additional services, despite the financial risk?

If you were the manager of a department and you discovered that an important high-level employee had spoken to a lower-level employee in a degrading and aggressive manner, what would you do? Would you take a firm position and possibly terminate a valuable, high-level employee? Or, given that this employee brings in significant revenue for the company, would you look the other way?

These are a few of the scenarios leaders have faced that we will discuss in the chapters ahead.

We all face countless decisions like these throughout our careers. The specific circumstances of the choices each leader faces will be different, but the core dilemmas and ethical challenges are similar. We must decide if we will we lead in the direction that's easiest for ourselves, or will we be like Julio and lead based on a strong set of values?

Many books have already been written on leadership challenges, often focused on strategy, growth, or competition. What sets this book apart, however, is a collection of real-life stories, experiences, and insights from boots-on-the-ground leaders, people who have proven that values-driven leadership actually *works*.

The leaders who share their stories here come from diverse parts of the business, healthcare, and education fields, but they all deal with the challenges of values-based leadership. They offer dynamic, living narratives that demonstrate the ways in which conscientious leadership, guided by personal values, can change people, organizations, and entire industries. As you read their stories, I encourage you to think about how you and those you are responsible for are affected by your choices.

I am a doctor who has taken care of sick babies and children for more than thirty-five years. I have also had the privilege to lead small teams, large projects, and diverse divisions. I have had multiple senior executive roles, including fourteen years as the CEO responsible for a staff of seven thousand, hundreds of thousands of patients, and a billion dollars of the community's money within the Gundersen Health System.

Today, Gundersen is a comprehensive healthcare network with a large multispecialty group medical practice, six hospitals, more than sixty clinics, a strong education program, a transport system, and an insurance company. We serve patients in nineteen counties in western Wisconsin, northeastern Iowa, and southeastern Minnesota. A wide range of evaluations have recognized Gundersen as one of the best healthcare systems in the United States

All that is wonderful—but the structure only matters because it provides the opportunity for Gundersen to do great things. In a highly competitive environment, we made huge progress in moving from good toward great in the services we provide the community. We have managed to keep our cost inflation lower than most healthcare facilities, and we made connections with community health long before it became a trend in healthcare. It makes me proud to be a part of Gundersen, but I'm even prouder of the vision and people that lie behind all these achievements. Our goal has been to improve the health and well-being of patients and communities that we serve. We believe in focusing on possibilities—not just obstacles—and we make possibilities become realities.

I want to challenge and inspire you with Gundersen's experiences. I also want to share with you stories from many of our partners from outside healthcare, people and organizations that share our values and helped us achieve our goals.

You will have countless chances to touch the lives of others, who will in turn touch others' lives, in a continuous ripple of positive change.

Although I am quite proud of the work we have done, you will also get to see examples from university professors, lawyers, business owners, and other professionals. These individuals have had the chance to touch the lives of others, who in turn touch others' lives, in a continuous ripple of positive change. As a leader—young or old, experienced or just starting out—your role is not so much about accomplishing tasks as it is about improving the lives of the people who work around you.

Lead True looks at leadership from four perspectives: self, people, organization, and community. If we were to draw a diagram for those perspectives, it would look something like this:

LEADERSHIP IMPACT

In the first five chapters, we'll focus on your values and how they need to be supported by courage, discipline, and durability. *How can you take on the world (or your department) and be true to your values?* We will talk about how courage, discipline, and durability can empower your leadership, making it not only stronger and more dynamic but also more effective. In the next part, we'll shift our attention to the people in your organization: *as a leader, what is your responsibility to staff, employees, and your colleagues?* Deep respect and real communication are the essential keys. From there, we'll move to the organization as a whole: *what is your responsibility to the entire organization?* We'll discuss how you can lead your organization's commitment to excellence and innovation, improving your quality of service and workplace culture. Finally, in the last four chapters, we will turn to the larger community: *As a leader, what is your responsibility to the world around you?* We'll explore ways leadership can improve your community's health and well-being—physically, socially, economically, and environmentally.

In the course of their careers, leaders make countless choices within each category. Each choice is a new opportunity to have a profound effect on the lives of others and to choose whether to use any leadership role to make the world a better place.

In each chapter, you'll see how each of these principles can help guide your real-life circumstances. My hope is that this book will both inform and inspire you—great leadership can make people, organizations, and entire communities better. As Julio Bird demonstrated, the goal of leadership is not to move one individual ahead of all others, so that a single person alone reaches the top. True leaders move *everyone*, seeking out the best route for all. When we lead true, we have the power to change the world.

The goal of leadership is not to move one individual ahead of all the others . . . True leaders move everyone, seeking out the best route for all.

PART I

LIVE YOUR VALUES

CHAPTER 1

CHOICES

At each fork in the road, your decision changes you—and the world.

The baby couldn't breathe. She had been struggling with chronic lung problems for every breath of her nine months, but today she'd reached a crisis and needed to be intubated.

The attending doctor fed the plastic tube through the baby's nose and tried to push it into her trachea, but it wouldn't go. While the baby struggled for breath, the doctor pulled out the tube and started over. Again, the tube stuck and refused to slide down the tiny airway. The doctor gave a heavy sigh and tried a third time. The baby struggled for breath and her skin was turning blue, a telltale sign that she wasn't getting the oxygen she needed. But the attending still could not get the tube inserted into her airway.

After multiple attempts, he finally gave up. "Okay, that's enough. I'll come back and try again in half an hour."

He then left the floor, leaving a group of frustrated nurses who knew that a half an hour could cost the baby its life. They turned to me. "Jeff, could you just put the tube in?"

I was an intern, only a few months out of med school, but the nurses knew I had far more experience than most first-year doctors and was nearly always successful with difficult intubations. Still, I didn't have a license to practice yet and, on paper, I wasn't the most qualified person to intubate a baby. Even if I were successful, without the attending doctor's permission, I would likely be in big trouble. I could even be thrown out of the program. So, there I was, facing a fork in my life. I could play by the rules and protect my future as a doctor, or I could step up and possibly save a baby's life.

When I got up that morning, I had no idea I would be facing a decision like this. Now, I didn't have time to ponder the long-term ramifications of doing one thing over another. The baby was dying and I had to make a choice immediately.

I decided to act and successfully put the tube in the baby. When the attending doctor found out, he was enraged. He said I was incompetent and wrote a nasty letter that went into my record. He also spread word that I was a danger to patients and unable to follow authority. None of that made me happy, of course, but the consequences to my career could have been far worse, and I had the peace of mind of knowing I had acted to save a life. Luckily, the other attending doctors supported my action. They agreed with me that the patient's well-being always comes first: ahead of a doctor's reputation, ahead of other people's egos, and even, sometimes, ahead of the rules.

At the time, I didn't realize that my decision was a pivotal moment in my career. I didn't think of myself as a leader in that setting; after all, I was only an intern. But by putting the patient's life ahead of my professional reputation, I was demonstrating an ability to not just lead but to lead with values.

Unless you walk out into the unknown, the odds of making a profound difference in your life are pretty low.

—TOM PETERS

Over the years, I frequently came to other difficult decision points in my life, places where I had to decide what was most important and which path to follow. The choices always mattered—they had an impact not only on my life but on the lives of others.

We all have those critical moments. Some are monumental, but more often they creep up on us in our ordinary daily encounters. Large or small, each incident questions our values—each asks for a decision. Even refusing to choose is still making a choice. Think of all the times you have disagreed with something but remained silent. Using silence to distance yourself from a critical situation is still a statement and an action. Silence is still a choice—one made in fear.

Decisions often involve risk, no matter which direction you go, and the choices you make will define you. Individuals and organizations will be remembered by what they do. Ask yourself, which route will make me proud when I look back five years from now? What decision reflects the best version of me?

GOING WEST WHEN EVERYONE IS POINTING EAST

Few of us get to be in the boardroom when high-pressure, high-stakes, corporate-defining decisions are made. How do leaders think in these situations? What do they value? What rises to the top of the priority list?

Walt Rosebrough, the current CEO of Steris Corporation, allows us an inside perspective through this description of a critical moment during his career. Although the pivotal decision fell to a small group, and ultimately to one person in that group, the impact quickly spread across a whole industry. Values drove him to act, and the action he took likely saved lives.

Walt writes:

> Back when I worked for a company called HillRom, the CEO, a man named Jack Clawson, epitomized ethical business behavior in many instances—but one story in particular comes to mind.
>
> In the early 1980s we were the most significant company in the hospital furnishings business, but we had many formidable competitors: Gulf and Western, which owned Simmons; Borg-Warner; and a number of smaller, regional players. HillRom, however, had developed and patented a feature in its premium hospital beds called Walkaway Down. This feature allowed the nurse to push a single button in the side rail, and the bed would automatically move from a high position into the lowest position—the safest position for an unattended patient. Since the caregiver did not have to stand and hold the button the entire time, this was also an efficiency feature. At this point, Walkaway Down had been on the market for about twenty years, and it was one of the reasons for HillRom's success. By the mid-1980s, though, the patent had run its course, and virtually every competitor had copied the feature.

Then tragedy struck. A child was crushed and killed in the mechanism underneath a HillRom bed with the Walkaway Down feature. After the investigation, we were all satisfied that this was a fluke incident; after all, this was the first time it had happened in twenty years of use, and there were tens of thousands of these beds with this system on the market. All our competitors in the industry and the ECRI (an independent safety agency) agreed that we should continue with the feature. So, we did.

Within a year or so, a second child suffered a similar "fluke" incident. Once again, the "experts" investigated and made the same arguments they had before about this being a statistical oddity. All our competitors—as well as the ECRI—continued the argument that the risk-reward ratio of Walkaway Down was appropriate and that the relative safety level was in favor of the feature we had invented.

We called a senior staff meeting to help make a plan as to what to do next. People from marketing, finance, and sales all argued that we must continue with the feature, because all our competitors, including the giant BorgWarner and Simmons companies, would be using the feature we invented. If we discontinued it, our sales could start to go to other companies who were still carrying it.

Jack listened patiently to everyone. Then he said, "We're not going to kill any more kids—period. We will not ship another bed with Walkaway Down, we will offer to eliminate the feature in every bed in the field, and we will advise all hospitals that they will be solely responsible for any beds in which we are not allowed to remove the feature."

As you might expect, the next few months were chaotic and uncertain. Our competitors continued with the Walkaway Down feature; some even went so far as to target advertising campaigns against our decision to eliminate it. We made our case, though, and the hospitals agreed with the decision on principle. In the end, we even prevailed in the marketplace. And no more children were killed by the Walkaway Down feature. Today I don't believe there is a Walkaway Down bed in use in the United States.

The statistics, the data, the competitors, and the experts were all pointing in the same direction. Clawson chose to lead our company in another direction altogether. Risky? Maybe. But he knew that we were going to have to live with our plan and the effect it had on the rest of the world. As a company, we said we will have the courage to take on the challenge of staying true to our values—even if that meant redesign, education, and new technology—rather than shifting the responsibility for children's safety to nurses and families.

The effect of Jack Clawson's decision that day didn't stop with children's safety. He taught me one of the most important lessons of my life, which has shaped my own leadership in the years that followed. And I wasn't the only one in that boardroom whose life was changed by Jack's challenge to put our values ahead of every other consideration. That is ethical leadership from the top.

You don't have to—or want to—wait until you have hundreds of people reporting to you. You can always apply the principles of values-based leadership. It is never too early or too late to become a values-based leader.

—HARRY M. JANSEN KRAEMER JR.

DEFINING PERSONAL VALUES

When we refer to values-based leadership, what are we talking about? Morality? Beliefs? Goodness? Certainly, values have to do with all of those. But those words alone aren't enough. They're not sufficiently precise for us to grab hold of as individuals. In order for values to become the foundation of our leadership, we need to be clear as to what our personal values truly are. A vague concept of moral behavior won't be enough to guide us day to day, let alone on a mountainside, at a baby's bedside, or in a critical boardroom meeting.

Values form our personal operating system; they are the internal programs that guide our priorities whenever we come to a critical decision. They are what infuse our leadership with clarity, strength, and consistency. Their source is often family, faith, or environment. They form a compass, without which we are lost when it comes to realizing our potential.

Your values may be personal and internal, but as a leader, you can't keep them private. To leave others guessing about your motivation when you make a particular decision does not build trust or clarity. Instead, values-driven leadership requires that you be completely clear about the values that inform and drive you and your organization's actions. It doesn't matter whether you're leading a department of eight or a company with eighty thousand employees, your personal operating system must become a consistent and transparent guide for you and those for whom you are responsible.

Values aren't necessarily positive. Your personal operating system could be that getting rich at the expense of others is your number-one priority. Or it might be that your personal power is more important than the health and well-being of those around you. I'm not saying wealth and power are inherently bad—on the contrary, they can be used magnificently to serve the greater good. But if your values are all about you, then you should probably stop reading this book right now, because that is not the kind of operating system I believe will best serve you or those around you. Granted, you may experience shallow, short-term success, but eventually the choices made will cause damage to you, your family, and your community.

The values we'll be exploring in this book ask us to look at the bigger picture: What will have the most positive effect for the most people? What will be the most durable and sustainable course of action? When you use these values as the foundation for your leadership, they may very well cost you something personally in the short term—but they build long-term, broad-based success.

We are all part of something greater than ourselves. We are inextricably connected, and our lives are interwoven with the people around us, the organizations to which we belong, and the communities where we live. Our actions create ripples that permeate these connections. Because of these connections, the decisions we make matter well beyond the moment they are made.

Organizations exist to serve. Period. Leaders live to serve. Period . . . Leaders don't create followers; they create more leaders.

—TOM PETERS

BUILDING A VALUES-BASED CULTURE

Gundersen is an integrated health system based in western Wisconsin, Iowa, and Minnesota, comprised of seven thousand staff, six hospitals, and sixty clinics. It has been cited by many evaluations as being in the top 5 percent in outcomes in the nation.

At Gundersen, we started out with some very basic, stated, and defined values: respect for individuals, excellence, compassion, innovation, and integrity. Everyone on staff, including the people who managed the physical plant, billing clerks, communications staff, nurses, and especially the senior executives, needed to be absolutely certain about the values that united us. We printed them in giant letters and put them on the pillars in the administrative area. We detailed them on our one-page strategic plan, we talked about them regularly, and we wove them into our staff evaluations. We also made sure that the patients, families, and communities we serve knew what our values were and how we had committed to living them. This had to add up to tangible, practical action that went deeply into everything we did and be consistent at every level—for individuals, small teams, and the entire organization.

A great help in our transformation was our human resources leader, Kathy Klock. She transformed our HR department from rules police to people-builders, using our values as their foundational building blocks. Our staff members knew they would always be treated with respect. They understood that they were working on something bigger than themselves, something that was making a significant difference in the lives of people and communities.

People will not follow a leader with moral incongruities for long. Each time you compromise character, you compromise leadership.

—BILL HYBELS

As an organization, we took responsibility not only for ourselves, our staff, and our patients but also for the larger community beyond our doors. We focused on the well-being of those we serve rather than just on our bottom line. We were flexible enough to disregard common practices when a different route created a greater good. That doesn't mean we didn't have rules or that we lacked structure—we simply understood that the rules and structure aren't important in and of themselves; they are just tools to serve the mission and reflect our values. We used them to build a better workplace and community. If the rules and the structure got in the way of greater success, then we considered it our responsibility to change them.

This structure and form must be able to serve us when the choices seem clear and when the choices are much more complicated. All businesses have increasing complexity as we get closer to the work and understand the implications of our choices. Dan Zismer, PhD, gives us his insights into sorting some of this complexity. Although this example describes complex decisions in healthcare, the lessons will apply to both large and small business and educational organizations.

Dan writes:

RUNNING INTO A BURNING BUILDING TO SAVE LIVES MAY BE ONE OF THE EASIER VALUES-BASED DECISIONS HEALTHCARE LEADERS CAN MAKE

Theologians and philosophers would argue that the nature of the human condition—left unattended by good parenting, cultural and societal norms, the law, and a belief in a higher power—will follow a predictable path of behaviors driven by insatiable personal appetites, self-serving manipulations of relationships and circumstances, and uncontrollable needs for self-aggrandizement. If they are correct, then those who exhibit the polar opposite of this profile operate from a value set that is likely constructively shaped by their environment and a nurtured personal belief system. Thus, good values are not innate, and value systems are not immutable; that is to say, they are available to be shaped by cumulative life experience and an evolving sense of self.

So how does this logic pertain to leadership, decision making, burning buildings, and ultimately the focus of this message, the US healthcare system? If values-based leadership is real, then values-based decision making by leaders is inevitable. Are leaders intellectually, emotionally, and psychologically available to a healthy and productive shaping of values as they mature into their leadership journey? Are they open to learning, self-awareness and reflection, and a maturing process guided by the assumption that values held today are likely somewhat different from those of the past and will be different from those held in the future?

Most of us believe that choosing to run into a burning building to save the helpless inside would be the right decision. I use the burning building as a metaphor for the biggest values-based decisions—those for which the right choice is obvious and the outcomes are irrelevant because the decision maker can stand tall regardless and say, "I would make the same decision again because it was the right thing to do at the time, given what I knew then." Well, most decisions that leaders must make are not black or white, and neither are they all right or all wrong.

This premise is set in the context of healthcare in the United States because the industry is complicated by competing incentives, politics and policy, the public good, and the need to make a profit in an industry that is, by regulatory designation, not for profit. This admixture of factors and incentives easily sets the minds and emotions of leaders reeling because the right and wrong of the next decision are rarely clear, even when set in the framework of a well-crafted organizational mission statement and values declaration.

Let's examine a few of the factors and conditions that weigh on the decision-making process in the everyday world of the healthcare leader:

1. Multiple, large-scale, credible independent studies support the assertion that upward of one-third of all healthcare consumed in the United States provides questionable value, while subjecting the user to the risk of avoidable physical harm. [As a leader, you are wasting money and causing harm in a system so complex that even the best make incremental, not transformative, care.]

2. The larger measure of the financial cost of services delivered is not the responsibility of the person who gets the services, and demand for many of these services can be stimulated by the provider. End users/buyers have the disadvantage of a considerable knowledge deficit and must rely upon a relationship of trust, where the providers/sellers tell the end users/buyers what they "need." [As a leader, how do you manage this moral conflict?]

3. Leaders frequently withhold information regarding impending policy change and market conditions that will negatively affect communities served and employees of the organization they lead. Release of what is known [a values-based decision] may harm the organization.

4. A sizable proportion of healthcare delivered in the United States is provided in the last six months of life. Despite a clear understanding of the inevitability of the outcome

by the professionals in control, the obvious and most difficult decision is often placed in the hands of those least prepared to make it. The question, "What do you want us to do?" whether implicit or explicit, is posed to families because steps that could have been taken to lessen the burden of that decision were not taken [advance planning, for example]. Consequently, high costs are paid by all concerned—emotionally, psychologically, and financially. [A solution to this dilemma is put forth in chapter 8, but it will cost you several times your operating margin.]

5. Upwards of one-third or more of the revenues earned by healthcare providers is paid by tax-supported governmental programs. Provider organizations [and their leaders] will argue that the price paid by these programs is insufficient to cover costs. Most providers cannot afford [morally won't allow their staff] to opt out of governmentally sponsored programs. Consequently, the business model requires cost shifting, a process that loads the providers' operating costs disproportionately onto private insurers. The result: double-digit premium cost increases, a large burden to all. [So do you unfairly shift the cost and save your margin, or do you not shift and lose your business?]

The examples provided do not fully plumb the depth of health-care leaders' decision-making challenges. They do, however, support the premise of the message: values-based decision making is not as easy as it may appear. Values held personally by leaders necessarily converge and sometimes clash with those of the organizations they lead, causing "values dissonance." Resolution of such dissonance comes over time as leaders mature in their understanding of their personal values and the role those values play in the decisions they are charged to make in the work setting. So, if the road to leadership maturity is paved with the cobblestones of experience mixed with the traits that make people who they are, then with each passing day leaders might expect to find the vault that holds their values to be securing a richer trove—one with greater utility over time.

What might be the lessons here? Values-based leadership [and values-based decision making] often sounds less complex than it is. Decisions requiring the applications of one's values are typically complex, meaning the answers to the related questions are rarely yes or no because "it depends." Fortunately for all of us, the human condition is such that we have the capacity to learn, develop, and mature in the application of values to decision making. We will however, need to recognize that in so doing, we will wrestle with the inevitable questions related to the connections and conflicts between our personal values and intrinsic motivations and the values of the organizations we serve. Oh, and one more thing: The higher the level of leadership attained, the tougher the challenge. And, I would add, the greater the opportunity to serve the greater good and lead true.

—**Daniel K. Zismer, PhD**, managing director and cofounder at Castling Partners; and Professor Emeritus, School of Public Health, University of Minnesota

WHAT DOES ALL OF THIS MEAN TO YOU?

Does any of this relate to you if you are not a doctor or CEO (or a mountain climber)? Absolutely. One of the most formative figures in teaching me values-based leadership was a small quiet woman who served as secretary at a Methodist church. She had never gone to college and wasn't the greatest speller. She was a pretty slow typist and was not really concerned about sentence structure or page organization. Yet she was *the* absolute go-to person for years at the parish when it came to advancing their mission. She was trusted by all because she was consistently honest and demonstrated personal integrity. She was appreciated by all because she had a genuine appreciation for everyone. Pastors came and went, but she held the group together and kept them on course. She treated everyone with respect and quietly articulated the values of the parish and where they should lead us. "Leading from any seat" was not a popular phrase then, but she was a strong, quiet leader, from a humble, values-driven seat. These were some of my first leadership lessons, and I am proud to call that woman Mom.

Titles don't lead people; *people* lead people. Not long ago, leadership and management were inextricably bound together by title and job description. A leader was a president of an organization, the CEO of a company, or the executive director of an institute. Managers were people responsible for planning and directing the work of individual employees. They were there to monitor all the work processes and take corrective action as needed. The focus was on individual leaders rather than on the people who followed.

Today, our understanding of leadership has evolved. Now the focus is on the entire group rather than on the prestige of the individual leader. We've come to realize that regardless of title or job description, all of us will be called on to make critical choices in our lives. In one way or another, we will all be asked to lead. The choices we make will have an effect on people and organizations far beyond the day-to-day details.

Good leaders don't tell people what to do, they give teams capability and inspiration.

—JEFFREY IMMELT

When we are clear about what is most important to us—and that clarity forms the foundation of every choice we make—we can more easily bring everyone else along with us. Clearly defined values are what allow us and those around us to make consistent choices when faced with important decision points. Jack Clawson, the CEO who recalled the Walkaway Down hospital bed, for example, was clear about the choice he faced, and because he knew what he valued most, he was able to define the path forward. He knew there were no promises that the path he chose would be easy or even successful from a financial perspective—but his decision was one he and the organization could live with and find a way to make work. The lesson and values embodied in Jack's fork-in-the-road decision not only affected those in that room, but it also changed the whole industry and affected the lives of many.

Values-based leadership isn't limited to those in executive roles. Every person within an organization or company will be called on to make values-informed decisions. At a bedside, facing a customer, or in a classroom, values guide each person's daily decisions and define what drives the organization they serve.

It is important to note—not all decision points are as dramatic as the ones I have described in this chapter. Your career may not be on the line, as mine was in the intensive care unit. Lives may not hang in the balance, as they did as Julio led his team up Mt. Everest. But that doesn't mean that your decisions are unimportant. To the contrary, when you face a fork in the road that tests your values, your decisions will trigger a cascade of consequences. You may not be able to see all the implications that are hanging in the balance; crucial choices don't always announce themselves. That's why you need an operating system that's already in place, influencing both big and small decisions.

In the chapters that follow, we will describe how there are three pillars that support the smooth functioning of any values-based operating system—courage, discipline, and durability. These three pillars form the structure on which values-driven leadership is built. They allow us to follow our values, keep our commitments, and persevere through adversity.

CHAPTER 1 TAKEAWAYS

- ☐ Our values define us and provide a constant guide to navigate fork-in-the-road decisions.
- ☐ Values form our personal operating systems.
- ☐ Values-based choices are often hard and have far reaching consequences that ripple through the lives of others.
- ☐ Our values are supported by three pillars: courage, discipline, and durability.

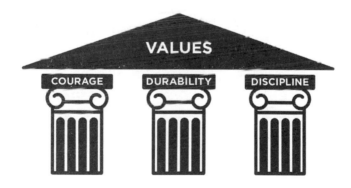

CHAPTER 2

LEAD WITH COURAGE

Courage doesn't mean the absence of fear; it means fear doesn't get to make your choices.

The child was completely unresponsive, yet her heart rate, blood pressure, and breathing were fine. The mother told us her daughter had become suddenly ill while they were eating out at a restaurant, and they had rushed immediately to the hospital. The doctor in the emergency department was puzzled and asked my opinion.

I started a routine, rapid overall exam. I slipped my hands under the little girl's thick hair to check her scalp. I had performed thousands of checks like this in my career, but this time something was very wrong. When I drew my hands back, they were covered in blood. The back of the girl's skull had been crushed.

The truth eventually came out. Irritated at her daughter for talking too much, the mother had slammed the little girl against the sink in the restaurant's restroom. The child had massive brain injuries. She died later that day.

Most of us feel compassion and even outrage when reading a story like this. That child was a bundle of potential, as are the thousands of other children who are maltreated or abused every year in our country. The phrase "children are our future" rolls easily off our tongues, and I've never heard anyone argue a contrary position. Despite our unanimous agreement, however, this statement is remarkably difficult to implement. Do we have the courage to do more than be horrified and outraged by stories of child abuse?

How would you respond to an opportunity to do something about it? Imagine if an organization that was doing great work protecting kids from abuse came to you with failing finances and asked for help. Now imagine that, by helping, you would undoubtedly be thrust in the midst of controversy and surely risk public embarrassment. What if your reputation, your career, and your finances were all on the line when it came to this decision? What direction would your values lead you?

When opportunities come along that require specific and concrete action, they are seldom easy. Even a values-based decision about child abuse may not be quite as simple as you might think. As leaders, no matter how much we truly care about children, we'll need to face our fears to find the courage to take risks that could have significant costs.

OVERCOMING FEAR AND SERVING THE GREATER GOOD

We faced this exact challenge after the economic downturn, when our finances were still a bit shaky. We were asked to take on a struggling organization—the National Child Protection Training Center—that had an outstanding mission for children; it also had the potential to be a great financial risk and a liability to our reputation.

A passionate attorney named Victor Vieth had founded the center on the premise that it is unacceptable that more than 1,500 children die every year because of child abuse or maltreatment.[1] Equally tragic, he believed, were the hundreds of thousands, probably millions, of children who are permanently affected by nonlethal but traumatizing childhood events. Abuse destroys families, and it snuffs out the potential of millions of children like the little girl I treated in the ER. So, Victor decided to take action.[2]

The action he took was specific and practical. He knew that doctors, nurses, social workers, and teachers had seen most of these children along the way—but these professionals needed help to identify abuse before they could intervene. To address that, he and his team developed the National Child Protection Training Center's program for members of the legal, law-enforcement, education, medical, and mental health communities. When professionals recognize the problems sooner, earlier intervention can prevent much long-term damage.

Victor's center had trained more people than any other organization in the country (more than a hundred thousand individuals); it had changed legislation; and philanthropists, strong partnerships, and a dedicated staff had worked hard to support it. But now it was in trouble. In a shaky economy, its financial backing was at risk. It would need to either drastically scale back its rapidly growing activities or close down altogether. This came at a time when the organization was training an ever-increasing number of people from around the

---

1   "Statistics and Facts about Child Abuse in the U.S.," American SPCC, http://americanspcc.org/child-abuse-statistics/

2   "Adverse Childhood Experiences," CDC, www.cdc.gov/violenceprevention/acestudy/

world. Victor and his staff asked several healthcare and educational institutions to bring the training center under their umbrella, in an effort to save their operations. But because of the fear of potential public relations and the perceived financial risk, no one was willing to commit to helping the center to continue its much-needed work.

Most would assume that leaders concerned with the well-being of the larger community would welcome such a strong and important addition to their organization. These weren't hardhearted industry executives, concerned only with the bottom line. Nevertheless, there was a financial risk for any organization that took on a struggling nonprofit with insufficient cash flow and a shaky business model for the future. There was also an even greater risk: attempting to prevent or decrease the incidence of childhood abuse sets you up as a potential target. Being involved in efforts to drag abuse into the light is liable to evoke anger and controversy from groups tied to places where abuse may occur. In the age of the Internet, scandals are explosive.

What would you do if you were in this situation? Most people care about children and want to stop incidents like the little girl I described at the beginning of this chapter suffered—but what if helping put you or the people around you at risk? Would you be willing to take the more impactful, but risky, way forward? There are good reasons—sensible reasons—to take another direction. As a leader, if you decide to follow your values despite the risk, then you will need courage to help live your values.

So, when the National Child Protection Training Center came to us at Gundersen, it was a difficult decision to make. Ultimately, our leaders decided that our mission to "improve the health and well-being of patients in our communities" meant having the courage to take on this organization and make it one of our own.

We could have given the organization an independent name so we weren't directly associated with it. Instead, we put our name on it. We said to the world, "This is the stand we will take. We have the courage to fulfill our commitment to the community. We will not back down from this opportunity to potentially change the lives of hundreds of thousands—or millions—of children."

If you don't have the courage to implement your values, they're just words.

THE MEANING OF COURAGE

Do you follow your values to their full potential? Or do you hide in the often-crowded "it's-not-our-problem" weeds? Those weeds offer you the opportunity to comfortably narrow your focus to the safe and the mediocre, while hoping others will take care of the rest. But hope is a weak strategy. If you don't have the courage to implement your values, then they are just words.

We don't always understand the concept of courage. We confuse it with fearlessness, when its meaning is actually just the opposite. If you're not afraid of snakes, then you won't need courage to pick one up. But if you're terrified of them, you're going to need a great deal of fortitude to be anywhere near one. Courage doesn't mean the absence of fear—instead, fear must be present before courage can exist.

Courage is also not the same thing as thrill-seeking—the craving for the adrenaline rush that danger gives us has very little to do with courage. A courageous person doesn't enjoy fear at all. They simply believe that something else is more important than their fear. In our case, our board and senior leaders were very concerned with the downside of taking on the National Child Protection Training

Center—but they didn't let their fear make the decision. They believed the greater good of countless children was more important and pressed on.

I've read authors who split courage into separate categories: physical courage versus moral courage. Physical courage is defined as the ability to face up to the challenges of bodily pain, death, or the threat of death, whereas moral courage is what gives you the strength to do the right thing despite shame, discouragement, or personal loss. Other authors divide courage even further into social, intellectual, emotional, and spiritual courage, in addition to physical and moral. Personally, I don't believe we need a different definition for different situations.

Merriam-Webster's Dictionary defines courage as the "mental or moral strength to venture, persevere, and withstand danger, fear, or difficulty." Danger, fear, and difficulty come in many shapes and forms, and to face any of them requires a consistent set of values to focus your mental and moral strength. When you come to one of those forks in your road where you know there is significant risk, it doesn't really matter whether it is physical risk, financial loss, or a possible blow to your personal reputation. You will need the same inner strength to call upon in making those decisions, no matter what is on the line.

COURAGE TO SERVE

La Crosse, Wisconsin, is a small city (about 55,000 people) in a small county (120,000 people). The community enjoys being the centerpiece of a mostly rural area of Western Wisconsin and Eastern Minnesota and Iowa. Strong higher education, beautiful Mississippi River Valley scenery, and relentless work ethic have carried the city through economic ups and downs. The city is representative of many small-to-mid-size communities throughout the US. Despite many manufacturing jobs leaving the area over the last decade, there was a rapidly growing company called Logistics Health Incorporated (LHI) that was truly a bright light in the community.[3] This company was providing hundreds of new, well-paying jobs to the area. It was equally important that CEO and part-owner Don Weber and his wife, Roxie, had become synonymous with growth and generosity. They had rebuilt a large section of the downtown waterfront where their business was located, and they were active in many other community initiatives. They were helping to lead the community forward.

The original mission of Don's organization was to help the government to more efficiently and effectively get our military personnel prepared for deployment. These young men and women often didn't have their vaccinations up to date, and most of their medical records were scattered all over. Don's company developed a system that saved the military money while contributing to the well-being of the young men and women in the armed services.

Early on, the company required an influx of cash as they were expanding their services. Don secured the millions needed from an investment firm, enabling the company's expansion. Things went well for about five years, and then the investors said, "Nice work—but now we want to take our money out."

This was a big problem. Don sought out other investors, but they all wanted to move the company's location away from La Crosse. Don had pledged to grow jobs in La Crosse and he still considered that to be a vital part of the organization's mission. However, the company was too big for Don and his senior staff to carry the investment themselves. What could they do? Give up and move out? Sell,

---

3   LHI, www.logisticshealth.com

take their money as early investors, and walk away wealthy but fail on their promise to stay and grow in La Crosse?

At that point, Don and then-president of LHI and former Wisconsin governor Tommy Thompson came to me and Jerry Arndt, senior vice president at Gundersen, with a very big question.

"Is there anything you guys could do?" they asked us.

"What are you thinking?" we asked.

"Well, we need an investor to bridge us until we can find a buyer that will keep LHI in town."

This was not a request to acquire a small organization or clinic. If we helped LHI, it would require taking tens of millions of dollars of our savings and investing in a non-acute care organization. We were being challenged to consider spending 20 percent of our savings. The stakes were extraordinarily high for us individually, for Gundersen as a company, and for the community. Despite the risks, Jerry and I felt that it at least warranted careful thought.

Our board was doubtful, but we convinced them to allow us to study the proposition. Several board members helped us, including a banker, a former executive from a manufacturing company, and a chief financial officer from a local manufacturing company. These were caring, thoughtful, amazingly hard-working board members who held their dual roles of stewards of the community and stewards of Gundersen firmly in their hearts. Together with these community board members, our internal staff, plus outside experts and council, we did aggressive due diligence.

We knew that any investment has a financial risk. More important to us, though, was the social risk. If we failed and LHI left, it would be bad for the community's spirit and economy. I faced personal risk as well, because as CEO of Gundersen any failure would be considered my fault. If things went wrong with such a large amount of money in the balance, it could easily cause the board to ask for my resignation. The staff would understandably be angry that we had wasted Gundersen's precious savings.

This was not an easy decision to make, but in a matter of two months, we studied, re-studied, and built scenarios. Personally, I became convinced that saving this large employer was part of our commitment to the well-being of our community. Eventually, we convinced a majority of the board to vote in favor of buying a portion of Logistics Health to save the company from moving out of town.

There was no immediate benefit to Gundersen. Instead, we gained a ton more work and risk. What we also gained, however, was the satisfaction that we'd lived up to our values. We were willing to face dangers in order to contribute to the well-being of many individuals and the character of the overall community. We had the courage to live our values.

Courage was demonstrated at the corporate level—but it had to exist first at the personal level. Without the commitment of individuals who were willing to step out and take a risk, this bold move would have never happened. Each of us having courage, one by one, added up to create something bigger.

COURAGE ON THE FRONT LINE

For years, Heather Armstrong had watched for job openings at the TV station in Bakersfield, California. Breaking into this business is hard anywhere but especially hard for those with minimal experience in California. Finally, through perseverance, she got her chance to interview—and she won the job. She would have to stay in a sketchy hotel until she found somewhere better to live, but she was so excited for the opportunity that she didn't mind. She was eager but unaware that from the onset she would face a critical decision that would require real courage to live her values.

Her first day on the job, Heather sat at the conference table with other staff members, pitching story ideas to the news director. He liked two of her ideas—so much so that he gave one of them to the morning anchor and the other to a more seasoned reporter. As everyone else in the station left to follow their stories, Heather was left sitting at the table. None of the other reporters offered to bring her along. They were a tough, competitive group, and they weren't interested in helping a new reporter.

Then, as the news director and the producer scrambled to think of some busy-work task to give her, the phone rang. The producer took the call, then turned to Heather. "I think I have a story for you."

The story was about the possible discrimination of a gay employee at a downtown store. "Go check it out," the news director said, handing Heather a tiny camera. She set off, excited, nervous, and desperate to come back with a story that would be on the five o'clock news.

After she interviewed the store manager, she knew she had what she needed to create an eye-catching news report. At the same time, she felt uneasy. The manager's words could be easily manipulated to make her sound intolerant and discriminatory— and yet, Heather suspected that it was actually a personality conflict going on between the manager and the employee and not a case of discrimination. Deep in her heart, Heather knew she'd been so anxious to get the story that she'd led the manager to give answers that made her look bad.

Back at the station, Heather's fingers hovered over the keyboard as she contemplated her dilemma. Finally, the news director asked her, "So, do we go with the story or not?"

Heather hesitated, not sure what she should do. She wanted to prove that she could do her job, but at the same time she didn't want to compromise her values. Her heart pounded. Finally, she answered, "No. We don't."

So, on her first day at her dream job, Heather sat and watched while everyone else put together stories for the five o'clock news. She had nothing. Not a single story of hers aired that day. "Maybe," she thought to herself, "my first day on the job will also be my last."

Finally, around seven o'clock, as everyone was leaving for the day, the news director called Heather into his office. "Why didn't you go with the story, Heather? Were you afraid?"

Well, yes, she had been afraid—she was afraid of not doing well on her first day at work. But at the same time, she was also afraid of hurting someone's reputation because she hadn't cared enough to get all the facts. She didn't know how to put that into words, though, so she remained silent.

"Didn't you think you had enough for a story?" the news director asked.

"Yes," she answered. "I did have enough. But at the same time . . . no, I didn't. I mean I had enough to make an interesting story—but not enough that was based on facts. It would have been wrong to twist the manager's words to make her look like someone I don't think she really is. It could have cost her job or put the store out of business."

"Why did you think you wanted to be a news reporter, Heather?" the news director asked her.

Heather's heart sank; this sounded like the lead-in to being told she wasn't suited for the job. Despite her fears, she said, "I have a passion for reporting. It comes from the core of who I am. I want to share information with people that can make their lives better, teach lessons, and get justice. But I did not get into news just to get a story."

The news director looked at her for a long moment. Finally, he said, "Be here first thing in the morning with more story ideas." He got up from his desk and opened the door for her to leave. "And Heather?"

"Yes?"

"Nice job."

Heather went back to her dingy motel room feeling proud. She had stuck to her values and won the respect of her boss in doing so. If she had gone with a story that was spun out of exaggerations and half-truths, she would have been left feeling terrible. Her story might have been on the news, but it would have been a cheap short-term win. She would have known that when faced with this fork in her road, she had chosen the easy route, rather than the one that aligned with her deepest values.

As she scoured the newspaper for more story ideas, she couldn't help but smile. She knew things had not gone great on her first day at the news station, and yet, in the end, she'd had the courage to stand up for the truth. If it had caused her to lose her job—well, so be it. "Better to lose my job than compromise my values."

This story does not involve potential loss of life, and neither were millions of dollars or the future of a big corporation on the line. But Heather's decision did effect the lives of others and the only thing she had to guide her were her values. It took courage to stay true to her values when a quick success at her dream job could have been achieved by ignoring them.

THE "FIRST VIRTUE"

Aristotle called courage the first virtue because it makes all of the other virtues possible. It takes courage to act with integrity; to show compassion to others; to act unselfishly, putting others' needs ahead of our own; and to speak the truth when it would be easier to tell a lie. Tom Thibodeau, professor at Viterbo University and director of their Servant Leader Program, gives us a great example of having the courage to speak the truth.

Tom writes:

The word *courage* comes from the Latin word *cor*, meaning heart.

To lead with courage is to lead from the heart. The more we are learning from the research in neuroscience and emotional intelligence, the more we are beginning to understand the wisdom of the ancients and their emphasis on the "heart of the matter." Do we have the courage to be warmhearted, tender-hearted in our interactions with others? How much of what we understand about service and leadership do we know by heart, therefore making it harder to be clear about our understanding of leadership? Have we met leaders or colleagues who have become hardhearted or worse yet, heartless as we have listened to their comments of decisions regarding the lives of others? Have we been in the presence of the brokenhearted and been moved to acts of compassion and courage? Is fear the enemy of courage or is it really apathy, the indifference to the anguish and suffering of others? Courage is always a step in the direction of compassion and justice.

I was fortunate to have a father who taught me about courage every day of my childhood. When I was twelve, he took my brother Mark and me to Madison, Wisconsin, to watch him argue a case in front of the Wisconsin Supreme Court. He was representing a widow living in the country. Her driveway was just off a county highway, and when the county raised the grade of the road, it became impossible for her to safely drive onto the highway. The county argued it was not their responsibility to provide safe access to the highway. Our father stood up for the widow and petitioned the judges to order the county to rectify the situation. My father had thirty minutes to state his case; the county had thirty minutes for their rebuttal. It was the hour that changed Mark's and my lives.

Our father stood and spoke for a woman who could not defend herself. He didn't have a legal staff or assistants. He didn't have partners to help him. The only tools he had at his disposal were his knowledge and research, a commitment to do the right thing, and a heart full of compassion for a defenseless woman. This is courage. To stand up to a more powerful entity—in this case the county government—and speak with conviction and for justice.

The following June, Dad asked Mark and me to grab two boxes, load them into our station wagon, and come with him. We drove out into the country and turned into a newly paved driveway. As we drove up to the farmhouse, an elderly woman came out to great us.

After we had unloaded the boxes from the car, the woman smiled and pointed to her strawberry patch. "Pick as many as you like, boys." She brought out glasses of lemonade, and she and my father watched us pick berries.

I realized later that our father had won a case in the Wisconsin Supreme Court and was paid with two quarts of strawberries. He taught us to stand up for justice with courage because it was the right thing to do, even if it wasn't always profitable.

Fifteen years later, I found myself in my own courage crucible. At the time, I was working at a residential treatment facility serving emotionally fragile and explosive adolescents. The center had an incredibly committed and dedicated professional staff, but in order to build the capacity to serve, a new leader with a prestigious PhD was chosen to develop the center into a national model.

Competence is often taken for granted because it's not as obvious as incompetence. Competent people do their work correctly, quietly, and easily. Incompetence is easy to recognize, though, and after only a month, it was evident that our new administrator was incompetent. He had no relationship skills, no ability to work with children, and no aptitude for completing necessary tasks, such as budgets or state reports. Complaints were common among the staff, and administrators were documenting what was not being done. But, as is the case so often, the incompetence was allowed to linger.

I knew it was wrong. This man's incompetence was hurting our work. I met with two trusted colleagues and after serious deliberation, we wrote a letter stating clearly our concerns about the incompetence of this administrator, which we presented to the executive director of the agency. The executive director was not shocked; in fact, he welcomed our letter and the courage it took to bring this matter forward. He said he had the same concerns but up until that moment, he had no documentation that was sufficient to proceed with the removal of the administrator. We were thanked for our professional display of speaking the truth with courage and candor. Action would be taken by the following week, he said, to replace the incompetent administrator.

That didn't happen. Instead, on the following Monday the three of us were called to the executive director's office and were each handed a letter stating that we were on probation for insubordination for the next ninety days. If anyone reported that we were speaking negatively about the competence of the administrator, then we would be immediately terminated.

Lesson learned: when you speak the truth with courage, you can be threatened and even punished. Whistleblowers and truth-tellers don't fare so well when fear dominates leadership.

We were disheartened but not discouraged. We had acted with courage and compassion. Our action had been motivated by concern for our colleagues and the children under our care.

Sometimes justice takes time. The law governing county highways was changed years after my dad defended that woman, so that the county or state now repairs property affected by road construction. An attorney who recognized my last name once told me my dad was responsible for helping to change the law.

And justice eventually came to my situation, as well. The incompetent administrator was found to have lied on his resume. He had stolen the identity of another person, and no one had checked his references. I was named as administrator to help clean up the disaster I had helped identify.

Courage in leadership comes from a heart committed to justice and rooted in love. All the virtues are interrelated, each dependent on another. Each values-driven leader spends a lifetime integrating the practice of virtue into his character and work. You never know if you have developed a virtue until you step into the crucible of discernment where the only way out is through. This is the work of courage, justice, and love. This is the work of true leadership.

Thank you, Dad, for teaching me so well.

Clearly, Tom Thibodeau knows what it means to lead true. In his case and Heather Armstrong's, courageous decision-making proved to be neither self-centered nor shortsighted. Likewise, the leaders at Gundersen had the resolve to take big risks for the well-being of a cause bigger than themselves or the organization.

Courage may be the "first virtue," but after you have found yours, your work has just begun. To have your values prevail over the long haul it will require a large element of our next topic, discipline.

CHAPTER 2 TAKEAWAYS

- ☐ Courage is not the absence of fear.
- ☐ Courage means not allowing fear to make your choices.
- ☐ Making a courageous decision puts vision and virtue ahead of your own interests.
- ☐ Courage is called the "first virtue" because it is the foundation for all other virtues.

CHAPTER 3

LEAD WITH DISCIPLINE

Discipline keeps you from drifting off the cliff.

One morning while I was preparing for work, the phone rang. The call would present me with another fork-in-the-road decision.

"Jeff," said one of our neurosurgeons, "I'm probably in trouble."

"What would you be in trouble for?" At this point, I was still smiling, but I wouldn't be for long.

At Gundersen, getting neurosurgeons who could do all the newest and most complex surgery, work collaboratively in an integrated system, and have great outcomes was a tall order. But we had a strong neurosurgical department of good people doing exactly those things. The young neurosurgeon I was talking with was a relatively recent hire who came with all the training, skills, and terrific outcomes we could hope for.

47

"Well," he said, "I was on call last night . . . had gone home and I just came back in to pick a few things up. I was there for only an hour. When I was coming out, I saw the security guy putting a ticket on my car."

"Where were you parked?" I asked.

"Oh, I was in the parking lot, but I was kind of over by the side."

I wasn't smiling so much now. "Do you mean over by the side where the fire trucks have to get to the building if there's a fire?"

"Well, yeah, but I was only there for a short time."

"You know," I said, "we asked the security guy to give tickets to anyone parking there. And after all, those tickets don't cost you any money, they just remind you to do something different next time."

The young man sighed. "I know, but I was angry at him."

My smile was completely gone now. "So you're calling me because?"

"Well," he said, "I hollered at him."

"What did you say?"

"Well, I told him that he should get a job that accomplishes something—something that's useful." He hesitated, but I was pretty sure there was more. Finally, he added, "And I told him I make more money in a week than he does in a couple months, and he should just get out of my face."

I didn't say anything for several moments.

"So," he asked, sounding a little uneasy, "I mean, you're not going to fire me over something like that, are you?"

This highly paid, highly skilled employee was way out of line. I took my time before I answered. This was a moment that called for discipline.

I'm not talking about discipline in the punishment sense, I wasn't about to scold or penalize the young man. I am referring to my self-discipline, the kind needed to have a thoughtful and organized approach to living your values. It's the self-control required to lead with courage. I had to decide if I was going to stay true to my values and our organization's values or let things slide for the sake of the potential economic impact we would face if we lost this neurosurgeon.

One advantage I had is that we had an employee compact already in place, something that already clearly defined our values. They weren't going to come as news to this man. He was already well aware of them. At the same time, though, as most people in management positions know, it's easy to make excuses for employees' behavior rather than face the hassle of confronting and possibly replacing a team member.

All this was going through my mind, but it was time now for me to answer his question: was I going to fire him?

"It all depends," I said. "It depends on what you do now. That part is not up to me. If you go to the security guard and apologize to him, and then you write a note to his supervisor saying, 'Sorry, I behaved badly. I was too hard on your staff member. I won't do it again,' and then, you commit yourself to treating everyone with respect from now on . . ."

This time it was his turn to be silent. I waited a moment, and then I continued, "If you can do those things—if you can understand why we don't accept disrespectful behavior from anyone on our staff—then you can have a long and successful career here. But you have to understand, when you came here you agreed to a level of behavior that involved respecting everyone. Regardless of your great abilities, you have to meet that standard."

"But I'm bringing in millions of dollars to Gundersen," he protested. "If I go back to my home state, I'll be able to get whatever job I want in any of the major cities."

"Well," I said, "if you're unable or unwilling to change your behavior, then you probably should go back to your home state—because you won't have a job here. You won't thrive here. Even though your medical outcomes are good, that's not the only thing that is required here. You have to take great care to respect our patients and our staff."

In the end, this young man decided to leave. He left a big hole that made problems and extra work for our remaining staff, caused a financial downturn for the neurosurgery department, and put stress on the entire organization. But it was a short-term stress compared to what the long-term stress would have been had that kind of behavior been allowed to continue.

Discipline was the tool I used to keep me true to our values. It gave me a careful, organized internal structure for dealing with yet another junction in my professional life.

THE MEANING OF DISCIPLINE

Jim Collins, the author of *Good to Great* and *Great by Choice*, has defined discipline as "consistency of action." Once you've had the courage to choose a path, discipline is what keeps you on course. It keeps you from wandering off into the weeds—or over a cliff—when stressed by economic or political pressure. Having courage is essential, but without discipline to follow through, those around you won't be able to tell for sure which direction you're leading.

Greatness is not a function of circumstance. Greatness, it turns out, is largely a matter of conscious choice and discipline.

—JIM COLLINS

Like courage, we have to define what we mean by *discipline*. It seems like it should be a good thing—and yet the word often has a negative connotation. As children, we may have associated it with being scolded or punished for some transgression we committed. As adults, however, we've learned that discipline can also be something that's self-imposed. Staying on a diet, for example, quitting smoking, or controlling a quick temper all require discipline. This sort of self-discipline is hard work; it often requires that we deny ourselves something in the short-term for a longer-term, deeper benefit.

Without discipline, courageous decisions will do little good, because they'll go nowhere. Discipline gives courage legs. If you look back at the stories we've told so far, you'll see that in each, the individual needed both courage and discipline. Without disciplined training, I wouldn't have had the skills already in place to help the child with the critical breathing problem. Just as Gundersen's decision to purchase the community business was bold, but the board would never have made that decision without a deep and disciplined evaluation. And without discipline, Tom Thibodeau, from chapter 2, wouldn't have been able to stick by his courageous action, despite the opposition he faced from management.

Without discipline, courageous decisions will do little good, because they'll go nowhere. Discipline gives courage legs.

Discipline is what gives you as an individual a values-based infrastructure that delivers predictability and objectivity to your actions. Discipline allows you and your employees the ability to measure how true you're being to your values. When you're falling short, discipline is what helps you correct course and continue forward. It makes the decision-making process regarding people, programs, or strategies far more efficient. You don't have to "reinvent the wheel" each time, because your values are already defined—and discipline ensures the consistent implementation of those values.

Consistency is essential to discipline. If, as leaders, we only have courage to follow our values half of the time, then those around us will become confused about our leadership. If we allow short-term financial concerns or political factors to prevent us from rising to the challenge when those moments arise, then the group will tend to hang back and wait to see which way you will lead them this time. They'll lack certainty and clarity, they'll function less efficiently, and they will not be able to make independent plans and progress.

Success is not a matter of mastering subtle, sophisticated theory but rather of embracing common sense with uncommon levels of discipline and persistence.

—PATRICK LENCIONI

THE CLARITY OF DISCIPLINE

We've discussed those vital moments in our lives when we are asked to rise to the challenge of an enormous but risky opportunity. In some cases, however, discipline asks us to turn *away* from opportunities, as Judy Faulkner has discovered during her career. Discipline is what gave her the clarity to choose the route that led most directly to her goals. It reminded her to not be distracted by circumstances that seemed positive and yet could have actually hindered her progress.

Judy has been hailed as one of the best IT company-builders in the United States, one of the most successful women business leaders, and a major philanthropist. The road to her success was not handed to her, though. Her greatness required not only hard work but also discipline and a consistent set of values.

After majoring in mathematics, Judy became interested in the rapidly rising utility of computer networks. Her work around a university hospital convinced her that there was a huge need to have more useful, broadly applicable, and effective computerized electronic health records. So, she used her skills and started a company in the basement of an apartment building.

Like many start-ups, one of her earliest problems was cash flow. She was always close to the edge of insolvency and constantly worried about paying her staff. Still, she believed in the business's potential. She knew that if they could just get through the tough initial period, they could be successful.

During this anxious and uncertain period, an opportunity came along for her to get a lucrative contract that was outside the scope of her work, involving billing and accounting in non-healthcare–related activities. She easily could have serviced that contract, and she certainly could have used the money, but she believed it would distract the group. Convinced that this contract would not move the organization toward its goal, she turned it down and stayed focused on delivering a great product. This took both courage and discipline, but she knew their success depended on her creating an amazing product. She wanted nothing to get in the way of that.

This became the standard she used to keep her on course as each opportunity came along; would it push her and her team closer to their goal or push them off course? She rejected any changes that added no real value, only distracting, easy money. She rejected many offers and lucrative contracts that would have forced her to change her business model. As a result, she slowly but steadily built what eventually became the fastest-growing and most widely used electronic healthcare records company.

She showed not only courage in starting a new business but also discipline in staying true to her vision. This is a key principle echoed by Jim Collins (mentioned in chapter 3), who would say you need the discipline to focus on what you can be the best at. Focus on what you can be either the best or the second best in the world at, and if you are not in the top two, have the discipline to move on. That requires courage to face the facts and discipline to act on them.

Judy was also persistent enough to stay true to another promise she made: to never sell the company. She wrote down the promise, talked about it often at monthly staff meetings, and let everyone know that her commitment to excellence and innovation wasn't ever going to be sold to the highest bidder. Her business is now worth billions of dollars, in large part due to her principled leadership.

Discipline doesn't only guide Judy's business decisions; the quality is evident in her philanthropy and family life. Her commitment to a disciplined, principled approach helped earn her recognition from the Smithsonian Institution, an accomplishment she is extremely proud of. A group of philanthropists had been organized by billionaires Warren Buffet and Bill Gates and asked to detail why, and to what purpose, they wish to help others. Her letter reiterated a lesson she had taught her own children.

As they got older, Judy's children became aware of how well-off their family was and began requesting more and more things. At one point, they suggested that buying them things was the job of a parent. "No," Judy told them. "My job as a parent is not to give you things; my job is to give you roots and wings." In her letter, she said that this was exactly what she aimed to do for others with her philanthropy. She wanted to contribute to the building of a values-based foundation (the roots) for individuals to help them go forth (the wings) and have an impact in the world.

It would have been easy to spoil her children and throw money at charities without much thought. But Judy applied a disciplined approach that sought to teach her children values and provide those in need with an opportunity to help themselves. Her practical and measured approach secured her letter a place in the Smithsonian.

None of these stories occur in the same settings or under the same circumstances, but they are all related in the way they showcase values-driven leadership. Every organization, department, nonprofit, or business of any size must face the struggles that will put their values to the test.

Dwight Klaasen, a biochemistry professor in the University of Wisconsin system based in Platteville, proved the value of discipline when he was asked to organize the university's planning council. He was faced with the challenge of deciding issues that had a large impact on the lives of faculty and students. Along with his friend, Professor Roy Smith from the physics department, Dwight worked out a plan to serve the values and mission of the school in a way that would increase trust and decrease the angst caused when staff found themselves in uncertain circumstances. Dwight and Roy focused on two major strategies. First, they built a sophisticated data collection model, requiring a rigorous investment of time and people, of all the current information on faculty and students—majors and minors, revenue and cost. This allowed for expenditures and accomplishments to be compared apples to apples across all sectors.

Their effort was not met with enthusiasm in most sectors. Facing opposition and negativity, they had to find courage to take on the old norms and the discipline to stick with their plans. Secondly, they created a giant visual room where all this information could be displayed on the walls (also a critical part of Lean management systems). Every department at the university had to use this room for their performance reviews and in planning for the future. Each department would be able to see every other department's results and use of resources. Data would be questioned, priorities would be debated, truths would be made public, and departments would be helped to find a strong path forward. As transparency became part of the fabric, trust grew, and the process improved in speed and effectiveness.

The staff, the students they served, and the university as a whole all moved forward more quickly as this visual display supported their consistent, disciplined dedication to a values-based approach to their goals. This work was not glamorous, headline grabbing, or dramatic. But the outcome built was a clear and trusted path forward that reflected the values they lived by. The courage to be transparent about the evaluation tool and the discipline to make sure it was both accurate and utilized properly was critical for its success.

Above all, success in business requires two things: a winning competitive strategy and superb organizational executions. Distrust is the enemy of both . . . High trust won't necessarily rescue a poor strategy, but low trust will almost always derail a good one.

—STEPHEN COVEY

Chris Hardie's thirty-one years in journalism is yet another example of how discipline connects us to the long-term embodiment of our standards. During a bitterly contested political battle that resulted in a movement to recall a sitting governor, Chris learned that two of his staff had signed petitions in support of the movement. Bias in a newspaper, he firmly believed, needed to be kept on the page marked "Opinion." Having it anywhere else would damage the credibility and integrity of their paper. When his staff signed on to work at the paper, they had agreed to sacrifice some of their civic rights to serve the greater good. As a values-based leader, Chris had the discipline to admit his staff's mistake publicly, take personal responsibility, and double his efforts to make sure his staff adhered to the ethical principles that support good journalism.

"The degree to which people trust you," writes John Manning, author of *The Disciplined Leader*, "is directly connected to the level of impact you will have as a leader." Leaders who are disciplined build trust. They inspire others. They create strong organizations. And together, they create change that is long-lasting and durable.

Be clear. Be consistent. Be your values. That's discipline.

CHAPTER 3 TAKEAWAYS

- ☐ Values statements mean nothing unless you follow them.
- ☐ You need courage to take the stand and discipline to follow through.
- ☐ A disciplined approach to living your values makes you, your staff, and your organization more effective and efficient.

CHAPTER 4

LEAD WITH DURABILITY

Durability carries courage and
discipline through the struggle.

Don Weber has come a long way. Once a homeless veteran, today he is a successful executive who leads Logistics Health Incorporated, as I mentioned in chapter 2. When faced with that critical moment when he had to decide whether to sell his company to a much larger organization for a hefty price, Don's decision was based on factors other than his own well-being. He knew that if he sold the business, it would be moved out of town to one of the new owner's major service centers—and people currently employed in La Crosse would either have to move across the country or lose their jobs.

Success hadn't come to Don easily or automatically. He experienced homelessness, failure, and bankruptcy. Selling his business would have allowed him to put all that behind him forever. But Don knew that to do so would also mean he had not kept his promise to himself and the community. Cash out and relax, or stay invested and risk losing it all? That was the dilemma he faced.

Don was clear about his values, however. He hadn't built his company for a big personal payout; he had built it to serve and improve the health and well-being of the community by providing well-paying jobs for its hard-working residents. Those people had trusted Don with their livelihoods—and Don knew the course of action that trust demanded of him.

I told you the outcome of this story from Gundersen's perspective back in chapter 2, so you already know the decision Don made. He turned down the payout and the guaranteed lifestyle that went with it and found another solution.

Don then committed himself to not only saving his company's existing jobs but to actually doubling them over the next decade. His legacy would be larger than personal wealth; instead, it would enrich the entire community. Hundreds of millions of dollars continue to come into that community through Logistic Health's payroll.

Was it easy? No, it wasn't. But Don has had years of practice at values-based decision making. "I try to always make decisions while focusing on something greater than myself," he says. Don has learned to recognize those critical junctions in life's roadway, and he has something besides courage and discipline—something that allows him to keep living his values over the long haul. He has endurance.

Courage to take risks and the discipline to make them work are a big part of Don's story, but those traits alone would not have been enough for him to survive the immense setbacks he's faced in his life. He needed endurance to do that. "My previous struggles," he says, "were a great opportunity for me to learn what's really important in life." Because his values are durable, they have remained strong throughout his life.

Don's durability separates him from many other leaders. His early experiences with hardship and failure might have taught other people to be greedy and selfish once they reached a more comfortable place in their lives; instead, Don learned courage, gratitude, and discipline. "As a person who once lived in a chicken coop on a cot," he says, "I have learned to be grateful for the simple fact of a roof over my head."

In chapter 2, Tom Thibodeau referred to the crucible within which our values emerge. A crucible is a container used to heat substances to enormous temperature in order to purify them by burning away all but their most basic elements. Metaphorically, a crucible's fire reveals an individual's true character. In Don's case, the pressures of hunger, homelessness, and failure became the container within which he refined his core values.

THE MEANING OF DURABILITY

Courage and discipline get talked about quite a bit, but the third essential quality—durability—isn't mentioned as often. This is the third pillar, along with courage and discipline, that supports our values. *Durability* means staying the course and sticking to one's plan and values in difficult times.

Durability is the power to persevere through hardship. It describes an ability to endure and remain strong. Like discipline, durability helps keep us on track for the long haul. Durability is essential for ensuring a constant application of our values. While discipline is an organized, external consistency, durability is more of an internal engine that helps make our values resistant to hardship and time. It remains true and strong, day after day, year after year. It endures.

As leaders, we often face a loud chorus of critics and doubters that threaten to break things down. You might hear things like: "Just this one time, it really won't hurt to compromise your principles." Or, "This situation is so small and inconsequential that it won't matter. No one will know if you compromise." Another argument might be, "You're so tired—and this is too *hard,*" or, "Don't be so idealistic. Your principles weren't meant for *this* situation. You need to be practical!"

Durability is needed to live your values outside the spotlight despite crisis and hardship.

Sometimes the loudest critic of our actions and choices comes from within ourselves. When we face these questions and uncertainty, it's durability that will hold us steady. It allows us to stick with the values we chose after that moment of courage, and it gives us the energy to follow a disciplined plan to live out those values in practical ways, regardless of critics, doubters, or conflicts.

Some people seem to just naturally have more durability than others. Most of us, however, need outside resources now and then to keep us going strong. Maintaining endurance is one of the reasons that leaders must gather the right people around them, people who will be able to support them issue after issue, year after year. Some leaders find this in their faith communities, others may meet regularly with a group of managers or executives who think like they do. Either way, those in leadership roles must find the strength that will keep them afloat when they are under pressure and inspire them when they are discouraged.

In addition, as leaders, we must recognize that this is an important part of our jobs, to give durable values to the others who also take on the responsibility to lead. We must find ways to continually give them strength, so that they can persist in following their values, even under pressure.

Values are the essence of who we are as human beings. Our values get us out of bed every morning, help us select the work we do, the company we keep, the relationships we build, and ultimately, the groups and organizations that we lead. Our values influence every decision and move we make, even to the point of how we choose to make our decisions.

—ROBERT RUE

STAYING TRUE TO YOUR VALUES

Often, sticking to your values means facing down detractors and not letting negativity deter you from what you know is right. Dr. Aparna Bole is a pediatrician whose values demanded she address the environmental impact of the healthcare industry. She was not welcomed as a reformer; rather she was scolded and redirected by those who felt such concerns were not part of her job.

Aparna writes:

I am a pediatrician and a first-generation immigrant. My family has always emphasized the importance of having respect for elders, and medicine typically has a culture that is very hierarchal. So, for me, it was particularly difficult to grapple with the strongly stated critical advice that came from my supervisors during my training, which ran so contrary to what I deeply believed was right.

I have long been committed to environmental stewardship, since well before I decided to pursue a career in medicine. In medical school, I noticed hospitals and healthcare facilities do not typically operate with an ethos of environmental responsibility. Our hospitals produce a tremendous amount of waste, use (and often waste) a significant amount of energy, expose occupants to an array of chemicals, and purchase food that is usually not sustainably sourced. The byproducts of our healthcare facilities can have negative health impacts on the communities we serve—an apparent contradiction to the Hippocratic oath healthcare workers take: "First, do no harm."

I grew increasingly convinced that greater mindfulness about the downstream environmental and health impacts of our own sector's operating practices was critically needed. It struck me that while kids with asthma were suffering more on days with poor air quality, the operation of our own building was actually contributing to that poor air quality. How could we just ignore that our practices were harming the very people we sought to help?

My pediatric faculty mentor was a traditionally minded, academic physician. I was honestly a bit intimidated by her. During a meeting with her, as I was preparing to apply for my residency, I tentatively suggested that I would like to incorporate advocacy for environmental stewardship in my career. She immediately responded negatively, telling me that this interest had nothing to do with being a doctor and had no place in my life as a resident physician or in my future career as an academic physician. She candidly told me that I needed to keep my head down and focus on being a doctor. "All this environmental stuff is extraneous—it's a distraction." As someone with a strong respect for elders, working in a hierarchal structure, it was tough for me to cope with this. Was it okay for me, a lowly medical student, to conclude that this venerable staff member could be wrong?

Later, at the end of my pediatric residency, I encountered another senior pediatric faculty member with similar criticisms. I had started asking questions about why there were no recycling bins in our hospital. After being told that most of our waste was medical, and probably not recyclable, I conducted a waste audit that revealed, unsurprisingly, that most of the waste we generated was preventable, recyclable, and often placed incorrectly in a regulated medical waste bin. The fact that environmentally responsible waste management can save significant costs helped me to secure support from our health system leadership for a coordinated effort to improve our environmental stewardship. At the time, as I was getting ready to graduate from residency, I was negotiating a faculty role for myself that would include clinical care and medical education, as well as a leadership position in managing our health system's new environmental sustainability program. That's when a senior supervising pediatric faculty member told me, disparagingly, that I was making a decision to be an administrator, not a doctor. She said that "this environmental stuff" had nothing to do with being a pediatrician and had no academic value. As a young resident, it was again difficult to hear, now from an esteemed senior faculty member, that my commitment to advancing environmental stewardship was seen as having nothing to do with being a doctor.

I made at that time what felt like a radical decision—though I had been taught, trained, and acculturated to the idea that my teachers and elders knew best, I decided not to follow their advice. Instead, I listened to my own conviction that the truth was in complete opposition to my mentors' opinions: environmental stewardship has everything to do with being a pediatrician, and environmentally responsible healthcare operations are critical to securing a healthy environment for the well-being of the patients, families, and communities we serve. At every stage of my career, this has been my "North Star"—the understanding that environmental sustainability and pediatric public health are fundamentally linked. Following that guiding principle has led to personal and professional satisfaction and more effective service as a pediatrician.

Now, several years later, things have changed both in my institution and the world of academic pediatrics. Our understanding in healthcare is growing to acknowledge that we cannot focus only on the 10–20 percent of a population's health that is determined by access to excellent healthcare. We cannot keep our heads down and focus only on the episodic clinical encounters we have with our patients, if we are serious about improving their overall health. Those of us who chose a career in pediatrics are ultimately motivated by a desire to help ensure a healthy future for today's youth, so that they can grow and thrive into a healthy adulthood. We now know that we need to think about the social, economic, and, yes, environmental determinants to health. And if our own healthcare sector's operations are failing to help support clean air, clean water, healthy food systems, a vibrant local economy, and equitable labor practices, then we are undermining our commitment to improving our patients' and communities' health. I no longer have to constantly justify why a pediatrician should be working on environmental stewardship in healthcare or why a pediatrician would care about advocating for issues related to transportation, urban planning, energy policy, and food systems—in fact, this work has become as much a part of my identity as a pediatrician as my clinical practice and contributions to medical education.

While I will always have respect for those who have gone before me in my profession, in my career I have had to, at times, reject advice when it was contrary to what I felt in my heart was the right thing. Sticking to what I knew was right has taken my career, and to some degree my medical discipline, in a fulfilling and wonderful direction. I am now engaged in improving community health, social justice, and environmental stewardship in every aspect of my professional life and in my direct patient care, administrative responsibilities, medical education, and advocacy. I follow this North Star in absolutely everything that I do and have been able to build a career out of dedication to a cause I deeply believe in. Making the decision to act on my personal conviction, despite some misleading advice from people I deeply respected, was the best career decision I've ever made.

Aparna did not allow tradition, hierarchy, or dated thinking to dissuade her from pushing forward. It wasn't easy, it wasn't comfortable, but it was courageous, disciplined, and persistent. Aparna continues to make an ever-expanding impact on the lives of many.[4]

---

4   Health Care Without Harm, www.noharm.org.

DURABILITY IN ACTION: THE BUSINESS WORLD

Obstacles, of course, are not unique to our individual struggles. The world may not be ready for your great idea just yet, but your values can carry you for the duration. Do you know the name of the company that had the fastest-growing stock from 1987 to 2012? I'll give you a hint: it was not Microsoft or Apple. It was Fastenal, a company started by Bob Keirlin that sells all kinds of nuts, bolts, and fasteners.[5]

Bob had worked in his dad's hardware store, where he saw an opportunity to improve service to their customers by selling their hardware via a vending machine. It sounded like a great idea with immense potential—except it didn't work. The technology was not practical, and the world was not ready for vending-machine convenience for nuts and bolts.

Bob could have been stubborn, led by ego, and continued banging his head against his vending machines. Or he could have given up altogether and gone into a different line of business. Instead, he stuck with the central core of his original idea: if he could improve customer service and make his products more accessible, then he would be able to sell more fasteners.

Like many start-ups, money was scarce, but he pooled his savings with four friends and together they came up with $30,000 to open the first Fastenal store, a thousand-square-foot shop in his hometown of Winona, Minnesota. By going the extra mile for customers and providing a level of service that kept them coming back, Fastenal gradually found its niche.

Bob later drilled his approach down to four simple words: *growth through customer service.* This motto guided him and his company

---

5   "Headquarters," Fastenal, www.fastenal.com/en/587/headquarters.

as they grew from a small regional supplier into one of the world's most dynamic growth companies, from one store to more than 2,600 and counting. "Along the way," Bob says, "we've aggressively invested in things that make a difference for our customers, continuously improving a multifaceted service network."

Bob goes on to say, "We asked ourselves what we could do better than anyone else. Well, we could hire people who were wired to serve. We could teach staff to listen to customers and sell only what they really needed. We could develop a supply network that was the most reliable one out there. 'Growth through customer service' drove our planning, our improvement methodology, our in-house university, and our relationship with our partners." Years later, when the company reintroduced the vending-machine idea, it was met with huge market-dominating success.

Being durable does not mean being blinded by stubbornness or a huge ego. Bob's genius was to keep the core concept (better service) and adapt it to the reality. At the least, stores would provide customer access to his product, which was the core concept of the vending machine idea. He utilized disciplined hiring and organization to focus on the well-being of the customer. He needed his vision to be durable enough to modify the basic premise and then stick with the plan, even after the initial idea wasn't popular. Bob Kierlin's values didn't fade away when the economy went up and down or when they experienced organizational setbacks. Instead, his values were carried by his durability and helped to set the course for long-term success.

DURABILITY IN ACTION: THE POLITICAL WORLD

The Affordable Care Act (ACA) has been a wildly polarizing issue. After the law was passed, the implementation of insurance availability and payment reform needed to be rolled out over a number of years, and it fell to state officials to try to make the ACA work for the people who had put them into office. Regardless of political persuasions, this was an issue requiring courage, discipline, and durability.

At the time, Karen Timberlake was Wisconsin's Secretary for the Department of Health Services (DHS). She describes the situation she and the rest of her team faced.

Karen writes:

When the Affordable Care Act was signed in March 2010, it was roughly nine months before the end of Governor Doyle's administration and my tenure as DHS Secretary. Governor Doyle was not planning to seek reelection, and the question we faced was this: What role should we play in supporting early-stage implementation of the ACA, given that we didn't know what the next governor's position would be on various aspects of the new law?

We chose to take a proactive approach to support ACA implementation by setting up cross-agency work teams to study the law in great detail, participating in multiple public briefings about the provisions of the law, and successfully competing for federal funds to develop a prototype of what has since become the insurance marketplace. We briefed members of the Wisconsin Legislature, participated in national meetings with the federal DHS and the National Governor's Association around ACA implementation, and held summits with key industry leaders to build awareness and ensure that the governor and all senior health leaders understood the industry perspective.

Our work was informed by a sense of accountability to the citizens of our state, our commitment to working collaboratively with federal and state officials and industry partners, and a desire to optimize this new law in whatever ways made sense for the people of Wisconsin. We received questions about why we, in the waning months of an administration, were working so hard to prepare for an implementation we would not be around to fully oversee, it was fairly easy to rebuff those criticisms by asking the skeptics if they'd really prefer the alternative scenario—to have government leaders sit back and do nothing for nine months.

Karen and her team chose a course that required not only courage to confront a controversial issue but also the discipline to create a process that would last beyond their tenure in office. They withstood criticism and carried out what they had promised when they took their jobs, serving the public good to the best of their abilities. While the media and the country was debating the law, these staff members chose to ignore the noise and do whatever they could to ensure the best outcome for the people they served. They could have coasted, knowing a new administration would be coming in and they would not be around to see the law take effect. Doing nothing certainly would have avoided controversy, yet they chose to take the more difficult road—one that corresponded with their values. They give us a real-life demonstration of how durability carries our values.

DURABILITY IN ACTION: MY OWN LIFE

I wish I could tell you that durability always pays off in success. Unfortunately, none of us has that guarantee, and individual success isn't the reason we stick by our values. We stay true to our values because we believe they have the power to make the world a better place. Sometimes, however, I have found that the durability of our values-based decisions may not always win the day.

Not long after I became CEO at Gundersen, I encountered a situation where I tried to set a values-based course of action in the midst of uncertainty. At the time, I had asked two of the most seasoned, most experienced, and highest-energy senior staff members to be responsible for most of our employees. These two individuals were smart and capable—each did a good job leading their own team. Unfortunately, they treated people on other teams very poorly. In fact, they actively hurt them.

I spent a great deal of time worrying about these two leaders and the effect they were having on staff members. As a leader myself, I tried to live and teach this core principal: no one's ego is ever more important than the well-being of the patients or the staff. The behavior and attitude of these two individuals negated that principle—but, at the same time, they were hugely talented. I convinced myself that with a little guidance, they would be able to align with our values.

It turned out that wasn't the case. As the months went by, I realized that I was failing miserably to change their behavior. Despite an enormous effort on my part and what I thought was great clarity, they disregarded my attempts and continued to mistreat each other and staff members outside their teams. Eventually, it became clear to me that I was standing at one of those crucial decision points in my career. I wasn't treating staff badly—but if I tolerated it in others, I would by default be supporting that behavior.

What you tolerate, you support.

Having failed to improve their performance, my two alternatives were either to focus on these individuals' talents and ignore their behaviors (since, after all, they were smart and skilled at their jobs), or I could urge them to find success elsewhere (since their attitude and behaviors adversely affected so many other staff members). I knew that taking the second course of action would concern the people who oversaw my performance, since these two individuals, in many ways, did contribute to the hospital's function and had been a part of its successes. Removing them from their roles would be disruptive to their teams and unsettling to other leaders.

In the end, I stayed true to Gundersen's and my own values, and both these individuals transitioned out of the organization. I had given them the opportunity to change their behaviors, but they chose not to. Now, they would have to find different paths for themselves.

I can't be sure what the long-term consequences of my decision were. If I had let them stay, though, I'm convinced that their behavior would not only have hurt other staff members but would also have damaged the credibility of my own leadership. Ultimately, it would have demonstrated a lack of durability of our values.

LONG-TERM VALUES

Whenever we come to one of those important intersections in life's highway, courage is what chooses the path, discipline is the system of actions that keeps us on course, and durability is the inner strength that resists the forces of time and conflict, giving maximum, long-term impact to the choices we make. Durability stays strong in the face of change and rises to meet any challenge; it gives us persistence, even when the road we're traveling seems hazardous and endless. These three pillars—courage, discipline, and durability—provide the support to hold up our values to serve the greater good.

Durability is strength and perseverance in holding true to your vision and values when things get tough. Together with courage and discipline, they form a foundation of stability—one which is able to support your values on any terrain.

CHAPTER 4 TAKEAWAYS

☐ Durability provides stability to your values, enabling them to withstand change and hardship.

☐ Sometimes our toughest critics are ourselves. Durability means staying true to your values and vision, even in the face of doubt.

☐ What we tolerate, we support.

☐ Courage and discipline require durability to ensure stability; together they form the three pillars of support for our values.

☐ No one's ego is more important than the well-being of the patients or the staff.

PART II

PEOPLE

CHAPTER 5

LEAD WITH REVERENCE

People won't remember your margins or your awards; they will remember how you treated them.

If you really want to see what is most important in your organization—what your top priorities are—take a look at how you acted during the last big economic downturn. For example, what happened at your organization during 2008 and 2009? Who took the beating? You reveal the strength of your values when you are under stress, not when things are smooth.

In healthcare, as was the case in many sectors, boards and leaders often went immediately to the biggest expenditure—staff. Layoffs solve the short-term financial problem. Many healthcare organizations then moved on to cut back services to vulnerable groups, such as mental health services, or they pared back education or community programs, despite the sacrifice of future benefits. Some organizations raised prices to again solve the short-term problem, regardless of the negative impact on those who are least able to pay. Some healthcare facilities even cut back improvement programs that would have kept them consistent with their stated missions of safe, high-quality care.

In the midst of the economic crisis of 2008–2009, Gundersen's finances were looking as shaky as many other healthcare organizations. When our senior leaders gathered around the table, many of them thought that layoffs would be a good way to improve our operating margin and make our year-end numbers look better. These were the same individuals who had helped put in place many of the tools we used to build a culture of respect for staff, but at this pivotal moment, the need to protect ourselves financially became a strong priority.

This was not personal self-interest, however, as is often the case, since we have no executive bonuses; our executives don't get paid more when our bottom line is larger. I knew these senior-level leaders thought they had Gundersen's best interests at heart—but I felt we needed to go back to our core values about whom we served: our patients and communities. To serve them well, we needed a strong, focused, and unafraid staff.

When I pointed out that all of us at the table made much more money than the folks in the front lines, it wasn't a popular line of thinking. The fact that we had not been able to anticipate and adjust to an economic downturn seemed to me to be a leadership failure— and that being the case, it made sense, I thought, to start the layoffs at the senior table. Since no one wanted to do that, we needed to focus all our talent and creativity on making us more efficient for the future rather than on deciding who to delete from the present.

The more special and protected we treat the executives, the less special and more afraid the staff feel.

My proposal? If we truly valued our staff, if we believed they were Gundersen's future, then we needed to treat them that way. I was convinced that affording special treatment to our executives, would ensure rest of our people would feel undervalued. The more we give special treatment to the executives, the less special and more afraid the staff feel.

To let staff know we truly were all in the same boat pulling on the same oars, we eliminated contracts for senior staff. This meant that they were truly in the same boat with their staff and that their jobs would be dependent on performance. Executive pay was average with no performance bonuses. Vacation and other benefits were modest, and to top it off—to demonstrate our humility—we renovated an old cramped space in the middle of the campus, where our office cubes would be easily accessible to our staff. As the CEO, I also worked in a cube, using an old conference table instead of a desk, my only cabinet a wooden exam table that had been rescued from the storehouse. We wanted to prove that we were not living in luxury while asking everyone else to conserve.

These weren't easy years. But any hardship we executives experienced was far less than what we would have asked of our employees if we had laid them off. We got through the economic downturn and we never had to delete important parts of our organization or lay off staff. Nor did we take out the cost on the backs of the community. The hardships had hit in the middle of a fifteen-consecutive-year period where our fee increases were less than the year before, and we continued that trend straight through the economic downturn.

So who did "take the beating" from the struggle? I did. I went to the board with no operating margin and received clear instructions on how I could not let this persist and that maybe I needed to change our plan and that these short-term numbers were just too unsettling. If you volunteer to lead, you volunteer to lead in the good and the difficult times.

Why did we do all this? Because we needed not only to respect our employees and the community we served but to treat them with reverence.

THE DIFFERENCE BETWEEN RESPECT AND REVERENCE

According to Paul Woodruff, author of *Reverence: Renewing a Forgotten Virtue,* reverence goes deeper than respect. In fact, he says, it is the source that gives us the capacity to act with respect. Respect, Paul indicates, is a set of cultural behaviors, while reverence is the "virtue that keeps human beings from trying to act like gods." In other words, when we have reverence for others, we understand that our interests are not the most important; we are not at the center of the world. In a 2003 NPR interview with Bill Moyers, Paul explained that reverence is what "protects the people who are most helpless from the people who are most powerful."

Respect is polite, often expected, and may even be required. Reverence, however, goes further. It allows for no excuses and no exceptions. Reverence means that if there's a cost to pay for staying true to your values, then you're willing to be the one who pays it. You take the beating—not the ones you are leading, not those you are responsible for, and not those you have promised to serve.

In the business world, this means rather than destroying the lives of the people who actually do the work, we as leaders are willing to let the profits sag briefly or take the financial hit if necessary. It means we are willing to do a ton more work to decrease waste and increase efficiency, but we refuse to pound the people who have the least power and the fewest reserved resources.

REVERENCE VS. PROFITS

Some of you who work in for-profit industries may be saying, "But we have to make a profit for the shareholders. It's our ethical and legal obligation, as well as a practical necessity." Actually, that's not true. In *The Shareholder Value Myth,* Lynn Stout quotes Supreme Court Justice Samuel Alito, "Modern corporate law does not require a for-profit corporation to pursue profit at the expense of everything else." Lynn goes on to explain that US corporate law does not—and never has required companies to maximize either share price or share-holder wealth. Companies' goals should, in fact, Lynn says, include growing the firm, creating quality products, protecting employees, and serving the public interest. In my opinion, chasing shareholder value at the expense of all other considerations stems from a short-term mentality that lacks courage, discipline, and durability.

Mark Platt demonstrated reverence in another business setting. Mark is an engineer who risked his job, a great financial payout for himself, and potentially his entire career to make sure that adequate care was given to the staff who had helped him succeed.

Mark writes:

> In 1995, I accepted a leadership role at a small industrial manu-facturer, primarily because it was an opportunity to be mentored by three men who had accomplished more in their long careers than anybody I had known. These men were planning their retire-ment and had decided to find succession leadership to carry on what they had started. I considered myself fortunate to have been

asked to be part of that new team, and I learned important values from them that became part of my personal mode of operating.

Several years later, after all three of these great men retired, I was leading the company with a partner. My partner managed the day-to-day operations of the business, while I drove sales, marketing, and product development. Through a series of interesting circumstances, the company had been acquired by a New York–based merchant bank with intentions of rolling out a handful of similar organizations with eyes toward a Wall Street initial public offering (IPO). As we were marching toward that goal, enjoying strong growth, profitability, and cash flow, our owner found a highly motivated strategic buyer for one of our sister companies.

It was 2000, at the peak of the dot-com bubble, and this other company had built infrastructure for the data-center market. This transaction, while very beneficial to our parent company, meant the IPO we were working toward was now off the table. Robert, my boss at our parent company, told me, "Prepare for an event of liquidity." Translation: "Someday soon I'll be selling your company. So, make sure you do everything you can now to maximize value so your stock options are worth as much as possible."

My immediate question in response was, "Why don't you just sell it to my partner and me?"

His answer came just as quickly. "Because you don't have any money."

Unfortunately, this was true. Robert did, however, agree to let us take a swing at putting together a management buyout (MBO).

The first thing my partner and I did, as we started down a path we had no idea how to navigate, was to decide what we would and would not do in order to get a deal. My top priority was to ensure that the thirty-five people who worked at our small but growing company had their jobs secured. However, my dreams of ownership also had a magnetic tug on my soul.

We knew the easiest route was to find a strategic investor who would take a majority interest in the company and then shut down our little growing local enterprise and absorb it into a larger operation. That would have been bad for our people and the community, though, and my partner and I made the decision early on that we would not put the company in a position that would potentially short-circuit the opportunity to build the business with the team we had in place, in the community where we had put down our personal and corporate roots.

We then spent months talking to banks, venture capitalists, and private investors. We found several local investors who wanted in and one interested venture capital firm that seemed to fit our values and priorities. The deal we put together had a trusted local investor group (which included my partner and me) in a majority position, while keeping the venture capital firm, which we did not know well, in a minority position. We were very clear with the venture firm that it would be a deal breaker if they needed a controlling interest. The merits of the deal were strong enough that they accepted our terms.

I still remember how excited I felt when it seemed clear I would own a significant piece of the company I had been running for years. It was definitely a high-water mark for my fourteen-year career. We had all the bank approvals, the asset purchase agreement with our existing owner, and the partnership agreements with our investors ready to go.

And then, the week we were to close the transaction, our venture capitalist friends changed their mind. Don, the managing partner of the firm, told me that for a lot of reasons (none of which made any sense to me), they had decided they really did need control if they were going to do the deal. They didn't want all these other private investors in the mix. My partner and I would still be okay, and we would still have the opportunity to make a lot of money. Don was sure that we should and would just move ahead in this new and surprising reality.

It was actually a pretty short conversation. Don was dangling my desire to own the business in front of me and expecting me to compromise my principles to realize a big personal dream. Unfortunately for Don, I hadn't been inventing my integrity as I went along, and I killed the deal. While I did not view it as a tough call, I was disappointed. I had spent a year doing two full-time jobs—running a business and trying to buy a business—and I had been excited about moving ahead as an owner.

I still wanted to continue on the path of putting a bankable deal together to buy the business, but Robert would have none of that. He was very clear that I needed to stop pursuing the purchase of the business (implying that if I did not, he would probably need to let me go). So, I did what anyone with a strong vision and integrity would do in a situation like that—I decided to try one more time to get it done!

I still believed the best chance to take care of our people was to have a local owner. And I believed in my gut that I could find a way. So, for the next six months, I worked to find replacement investors and a replacement bank (the venture capital firm poisoned the bank deal we previously had)—and I did it on my own time. Once the pieces were in place, I made a nervy call to Robert to convince him that the deal really was done this time.

We closed the transaction several months later. The company stayed in the area and thrived. I remained in the position of president and CEO of the organization for another ten years, while we enjoyed tenfold growth. I was very fortunate to have had the opportunity to lead a great group of people through a very special time.

As I look back, I really was making it up as I went along. I had never before been on the path that I found myself walking during those two years. I stumbled into some pretty good stuff, you might say by accident, but at the same time I was intentional about every step. I knew why winning was important, and it was for something bigger than myself.

I thank the men who mentored me for teaching me the value of the people who work for me.

Mark would have had a much easier path to take the cash and allow the company to get sold, break up, or struggle along. However, he was driven by a deep conviction that he also had a responsibility to the staff whom he worked with. He believed there was a higher calling than just taking the money and securing his future. Living his values pushed him to choose the more difficult course and to persevere in the face of great obstacles and escalating risk.

REVERENCE

So, what does treating your staff with not just respect but also with reverence look like? We felt our role was not to make our staff member's lives easy but to help them to understand and to find a path to both personal well-being and professional success. We broke this down into four steps:

1. Define the work.

2. Describe the path for individual and team success.

3. Ensure that staff members have the training, tools, and environment they need to succeed.

4. Build your leaders.

DEFINE THE WORK

At Gundersen, we make sure that we define our values starting with our very first contact with our employees, during the applications process. On our electronic and printed applications and website material, we are candid and clear about what we expect: integrity, compassion, excellence, and respect for all. We make clear that we will not settle for mediocrity. We clearly impart that these are not just words on the wall but apply to everyone all the time. It is clear we are a great, but hard, place to work.

If you work for Gundersen, you will be asked to live by those values, to press for excellence, to treat even people you don't like with respect, and to serve a purpose bigger than yourself. We knew that providing a clear, albeit difficult, path forward would help us find staff that would take the challenge to excel in a demanding, yet values-driven, environment that serves a greater good.

DESCRIBE THE PATH FORWARD

Job descriptions and values statements are a good start but won't create a great values-driven culture. As seen in the applicant phase, there is a dual responsibility of what the staff member and the organization need to deliver on. We codified those mutual expectations with a social agreement called a *compact*. A compact can be a powerful transformative skill. It clearly lays out the responsibility of both the organization and the staff in a way that is clear, concise, and able to be used as a way to gauge performance.

We gave the compact to staff when they applied and again when they joined the team. This helps to build an environment where expectations are clear for all and consistently point everyone toward the values of the organization.

Here's what it looks like:

MEDICAL STAFF COMPACT

GUNDERSEN HEALTH SYSTEM'S RESPONSIBILITIES	MEDICAL STAFF'S RESPONSIBILITIES
ACHIEVE EXCELLENCE	**FOCUS ON SUPERIOR PATIENT CARE**
· Recruit and retain outstanding physicians and staff	· Practice evidence-based, high-quality medicine
· Support career development and enhance professional satisfaction	· Encourage increased patient understanding, involvement in care, and treatment decisions
· Acknowledge and reward superior performance that enhances patient care and improves Gundersen Health System	· Achieve and maintain optimal patient access
	· Insist on departmental focus on superior patient service
· Create opportunities to participate in quality improvement, research, and improvements in community health	· Work in collaboration with other physicians, support staff and management across the system in both service and patient care improvements
COMMUNICATION	· Demonstrate the highest levels of integrity and professional conduct
· Communicate information regarding organizational priorities, business decisions, and strategic plans	· Participate in or support education and research
· Provide opportunities for constructive dialogue, clarity of goals, and regular evaluation	**TREAT ALL PEOPLE WITH RESPECT**
EDUCATE	· Listen and communicate both clinical and non-clinical information in a clear, respectful, and timely manner
· Support and facilitate teaching and learning opportunities	· Provide and accept feedback in a respectful manner from all staff and outside contacts
· Provide the tools necessary to continually improve medical practice	**TAKE OWNERSHIP**
REWARD	· Provide leadership to improve outcomes quality and service quality
· Provide competitive compensation consistent with market values and organizational goals of quality, service, and efficiency	· Work to ensure personal, departmental, and organizational compliance with all legal and educational requirements
· Maintain clear organizational responsibility and integrity to those it serves	· Steadily improve the efficiency and economic aspects of your practice
CHANGE	**CHANGE**
· Manage the inevitable rapid changes in healthcare so that staff have an opportunity for participation, for clarity of goals, and continuous modification of the process as well as the outcomes	· Embrace innovation to continuously improve patient care, service and organizational efficiency

GUNDERSEN
HEALTH SYSTEM®
Where Caring Meets Excellence

Gundersen Lutheran Medical Center, Inc. | Gundersen Clinic, Ltd.

ENSURE THAT STAFF HAVE THE TRAINING, TOOLS, AND ENVIRONMENT TO SUCCEED

Staff training sounds rather mundane, but it is a great separator between mediocre and great organizations. To truly match the needs of the work with the right technical and social skills, in a rapidly changing environment, and to do so in an efficient and effective manner is no small accomplishment. Those who provide lip service and superficial attention to these concepts will pay for it in a less capable, but more importantly, less engaged workforce.

An important piece of our plan that demonstrated a deeper respect for people was to use an improvement process and tools that honored their insight, input, and problem-solving abilities. First was the Change Acceleration Process (CAP) from General Electric. CAP is an organized, staff-honoring approach that emphasized why we needed to change *with* the staff, rather than issuing top-down edicts. We coupled that with many of the principals from *Lean* management and improvement systems. Championed in healthcare by John Toussaint, *Lean* is a system that focuses on decreasing system waste, rather than individuals' deficiencies. It truly is a disciplined, people-focused approach that can help you build a more inclusive culture.[6]

We will talk about leadership behaviors in the next section, but an example of how it is organized is seen with one of its many tools that are both people building and problem solving. The A3 planning process refers to a team-based approach to defining current state, future state, and barriers and building a plan forward to test and modify. And all this is done on one sheet of A3 paper—a paper size that is slightly longer but less wide than 11x17–inch paper. The

---

6   John Toussaint, "The Lowdown on Lean Healthcare," interview by Roberto Priolo, *Planet Lean*, January 12, 2016, http://planet-lean.com/john-toussaint-on-lean-thinking-in-healthcare.

paper is not the focus; it is engaging the staff to be a part of identifying the problem and its solution. The purpose of the A3 process is to help groups work together on in-depth problem solving to achieve common goals. It allows for a system of ongoing improvement, clarity of progress, and provides opportunity to be recognized for being an important part of accomplishing our mission.

Respect is being thoughtful about the communication of change; *reverence* engages staff in a respectful use of their talents to foster change.

As mentioned, one of the first tasks with an A3 is to describe the current state, how things are functioning or not functioning now. It doesn't matter if we're talking about dietary aids, long-term housekeeping staff, or senior medical staff—they all love describing the current state. They are glad you asked! Next, ask them what would an ideal state look like? It is easy to get them engaged and easy for them to feel they can be a part of the solution. Now imagine you have people from several different departments all describing what they see as current state and ideal solutions. Not only do you have enthusiasm, but you also get a real understanding of how they all view the organization.

All of these tools are good, but *great* would mean you had a continuous system of reevaluation assessing whether changes make a difference. Are there more unmet needs? To address this, to ensure that the improvement held and the staff could see substance and persistence to their changes, we finished off our approach with a continuous PDSA cycle (Plan, Do, Study, Act), learned from the Institute for Healthcare Improvement (IHI), although this concept is used across businesses and industries. The staff come to know this cycle: expect the change, help suggest the change, and track the progress on large visual boards open for all to see.

Respect is letting staff do something; *reverence* is developing a system that shows they made a meaningful, long-lasting change.

As a final feature, every Friday we have an improvement event to call out improvement successes or failures, so that all can learn. Attended by senior staff and mid-level leaders, these are great opportunities for frontline staff to proudly display their work and receive direct praise from the CEO and senior staff. Everyone learns, and everyone feels they are a part of an organization that is moving forward and appreciates the work, regardless of the title. This deepens the bond between mission, values, and the staff.

Of course, such a system can markedly speed up improvement and organization. Far more important is the effect it can have on the staff. If done well, they are given the tools and opportunity to share their knowledge, be part of improving outcomes, grow as individuals, and learn as a team. It's hard work, but it creates great personal growth and a deeper connection to the mission and values of the organization.

Not finance. Not strategy. Not technology. It is teamwork that remains the ultimate competitive advantage, both because it is so powerful and so rare.

—PATRICK LENCIONI

BUILD YOUR LEADERS

If you inspire your staff (your mission and goals), give them a consistent and positive path forward (the compact), and provide useable tools that help them know they are making a difference (CAP, A3, PDSA), it is a great start, but it doesn't end there. It won't win them long-term, deep respect. A major piece is the training, building, and managing of leaders. Staff may join a company for the opportunity, but research points out they often become disengaged, or leave, because of their manager.

As pointed out earlier, our approach to staff development was to be people-builders, not rules police. We were clear about the expectations, were clear about what skills and competencies were needed to succeed in that role, and worked very hard to give them every chance to grow.

Sounds good, but how do you avoid silos of senior leaders doing their own thing? How do you ensure fair evaluation and limit friends promoting friends? How do you organize yourself to allow all leaders to be developed rather than policed?

The stakes are very high. What is viewed by the top as minor variation, in the trenches is major aberration. If we remember to work hard to understand what the work and the senior staff behavior looks like from a different position, we will have a better environment for staff, and the leaders of the organization will be thought of as living more consistent with our values.

The problem is how to develop this consistent approach to leader development. We had a very in-depth program that included selection, education, and competencies. One of the less-common parts of our program was again borrowed from outside our industry. We used GE's *9 Box System* to be more disciplined on how we developed our leaders.

Here's a quick description on how it was used. If you were a director, at a meeting of the most senior leaders, your vice president would place your name in one of the squares and explain why they thought you were performing great and what your potential was. The other vice presidents (including the VP of HR) and the CEO would have a chance to ask questions, relate their experience with you and your performance, comment on characters outside of the team, and suggest opportunities for all to help in your development. The discussions are positive but honest. If you behaved well around your VP, who was also your close friend and close mentor, but treated others poorly, it came out. A plan would be made to work on that. If you were judged harshly by your leader, and yet all the other leaders had seen you perform well in many other settings, that also came out and would be addressed.

The progress and plans, as well as the struggles and needs for all the rising leaders, were known by all of the senior leaders. It was made the responsibility of all to help each of these developing staff members, regardless of what team they were on. The impact on those being discussed was potentially great. The impact on their staff was probably even greater. You can't build a great place to work, you can't treat staff with ever-deepening respect and reverence unless you have the courage to take on leadership performance and behavior issues. All the speeches, banners, celebrations, and prizes won't result in great staff performance if you allow poor performance by leaders anywhere in the organization.

You cannot give what you do not have. If the staff doesn't feel cared for, then they can't care for others properly—to embrace, you have to have been embraced. To respect, you have to have been respected. If your staff does not feel they have been cared for, respected, and connected with, don't be stunned by their lack of care, connection, or respect.

—MAUREEN BIGANANO

Another integral part is having the discipline to manage bad actors, whether they are in prominent positions or not. In chapter 3, I talked about the neurosurgeon who could not come to grips with treating everyone with respect. Although we have very high quality standards, we have had to dismiss more clinicians for behavior than technical competence. These are always painful, disruptive, and hard on the individual and their family, as well as on our staff and their partners.

Our first move is always to understand the situation, try to improve the system, as well as the staff person's understanding of expectations, and then provide them with multiple avenues and opportunities to get better. Sometimes it is a process issue, sometimes a culture issue, and sometimes it's a matter of adjusting to a new set of expectations. We are extremely flexible on how to improve and where to get help—doing it onsite or going to conferences or training programs as needed. We are not flexible at all on the outcomes, however. Despite the short-term disruption, or how hard it might be to replace, the long-term advantage of removing a toxic staff member, clinician, or administrator markedly outweighs the short-term issues. We need to have the courage to address these critical issues that fall the hardest on those in the most vulnerable positions. Not addressing them abdicates our responsibility as a leader and supports a much different set of values.

REVERENCE AND HUMILITY

Woodruff's definition of reverence as the virtue that keeps us from "trying to act like gods," underlines one of the essential qualities inherent to reverence: humility. A senior vice president at Gundersen, Jerry Arndt, had also been a high-level executive in a competitive manufacturing business. He shares his story of how humility shaped his concept of leadership.

Jerry writes:

Out of basic necessity, during the first two weeks of my professional career, I learned a leadership value that defined my leadership style throughout my entire forty-five-year career. That value is "humility in leadership," and it became more deeply rooted at each stage of my career as I climbed the leadership ladder to higher levels.

When I graduated from college in 1970, I went to work as a manufacturing engineer at Trane Company, a worldwide leader in commercial air-conditioning equipment. Based on my college performance and the "sunshine" that recruiters had pumped into me, it never occurred to me that I might not be ready for my first assignment at Trane.

Well, I learned very quickly that I was not ready. My first assignment involved the development of a manufacturing process to produce a proprietary patented heat exchanger product to reduce the material content and reduce the cost of several Trane products. Trane had patents on the design but did not have the manufacturing technology to produce it; it was my job to develop that capability. Because it was something totally new, there was very little "state-of-the-art" for me to apply. I felt pretty helpless.

After struggling for a short time, I had one of those blinding flashes of the obvious: maybe some production workers in the factory or tool-and-die makers in the tool room might be able to help me. After all, they were the ones who really understood the existing processes and the technology that my project would replace. I asked several of these folks if they would be willing to let me join them for lunch for a few days in the factory lunch room to chat about my project. They reluctantly agreed; I suspect they expected to hear some new hotshot engineer talking down to them, telling them what I was going to do and how it would change their jobs.

Instead, I gave them a sincere and genuine plea for help. And they were awesome. Because of them, the project was a big success. I made absolutely sure that they were recognized and credited for the success.

That was my first lesson in humility. More than twenty years later in my career at Trane, when I had advanced to an executive leadership role, I got another lesson when I faced the challenge of leading through some very difficult and strained labor-management relations.

An ugly strike in 1991 had the potential to end the manufacturing presence of Trane in La Crosse, Wisconsin, where the company was founded in the late 1800s. That strike followed a series of strikes that had occurred every six years (every other contract negotiation) for several cycles prior to 1991. As a result, the labor–management tension was steadily shrinking the manufacturing presence in La Crosse, as management transferred products one at a time to other locations. So at the conclusion of that 1991 strike, I gathered the factory management people and the union leaders on a memorable Sunday evening for a state-of-the-business meeting that occurred each year.

Typically, those meetings were pretty much a monologue presentation from management about business data (quality, market share, product plans, financial performance, etc.). There were usually many transparencies projected from an overhead projector (few will remember those days) that included all the stuff that made it an official business meeting. Most of the audience endured this simply because it was a necessary step to the social hour and dinner that followed the presentation.

The meeting in 1991 was different. I got up in front of the group and told them that I only had one slide: a graph that showed the steady decline in the unionized factory workforce that had occurred over the last decade and the linkage between the workforce numbers and the products that had already been transferred out of La Crosse. I pointed out that all the remaining La Crosse products were scheduled for redesign over the life of the contract they had just struck to get. I told them I wasn't asking for anything from them, but I felt responsible to point out what might be in their future. Without me saying much more, they knew that the contract would not bode well for keeping those products in La Crosse.

Then I turned the lights in the room back on. "I have nothing else to say," I told them, "unless you have any questions or comments."

For a moment, there was deafening silence—and then the questions came: what could they do to change the situation?

My "humility in leadership" approach required that I not be prescriptive and demanding about what the union needed to do, but rather to demonstrate that I wanted to work together in a "guided discovery" approach to find a win-win arrangement. I reemphasized that I didn't have any answers and I wasn't making any demands. I did offer to work with them and help them if there was anything they wanted me to do.

By the end of the next workday on Monday, the message had gone through most of the workforce. A few days later, the union leadership approached me about negotiating an amendment to the contract. Fortunately, we were able to agree on a contract amendment that wound up being a big win-win. Even better, the negotiation approach that was used to reach the agreement set the negotiation tone for many years that followed. There has not been a work stoppage in La Crosse since 1991, and the workforce has stabilized, with new products in production.

The trust that was developed during the process carried over to the way we ran the business in other matters. The total turn-around we experienced led to Trane La Crosse being selected as the 1996 Wisconsin Manufacturer of the year. When we received the award, I invited the union leadership to come forward to the stage along with the company's management team. Together, we emphasized labor–management collaboration as the key ingredient to the success of Trane-La Crosse.

As my responsibilities at Trane grew from project management to team management to department management to business unit management and eventually to executive leadership, I realized more and more that I had people in my down-line that were much stronger experts and probably much smarter than me about the work and the product. I needed my people more than they needed me.

So what was my role? My role as a leader, I came to understand, was to create the right environment for my teammates to feel needed, appreciated, and empowered to do what needed to be done—and to be as good as they could be in helping the team achieve its goals and objectives. My role was to create a "team chemistry" that recognized that each team member was unique and brought something different to the team. My role was to eliminate barriers. My role was to take the hits for the team when things didn't always go well and to give the credit to my teams when things were successful.

I have found that humility in leadership manifests itself in so many ways. Some may seem small and insignificant and yet often have huge impacts on my relationships with the people I lead. Some of the best ideas and most meaningful contributions came from people who were comfortable approaching me, knowing that their input was sincerely appreciated.

In reflecting on my forty-five-year career, I recognize that my understanding of humility in leadership may not look like what others would consider leadership to be.

To clarify what humility in leadership isn't. It isn't:

- weakness as a leader

- lack of confidence

- lack of pride

- uncertainty and indecisiveness

- being ashamed of your vulnerabilities

- letting yourself get manipulated or pushed around by your people or other external forces

So what is humility in leadership? It is:

- self-awareness, acknowledging to yourself and others that you don't always know all the answers

- willingness to expose your personal vulnerabilities and knowledge gaps to the people you are leading

- realizing and acknowledging that you may not be the best player on the team and you don't have to be—

> because making your team better than what you could be yourself is what leadership is all about.
>
> □ willingness to learn
>
> □ willingness to admit when you are wrong and a willingness to change direction when that is necessary
>
> □ willingness to personally accept responsibility for failures and setbacks that your team experiences without trying to deflect blame or criticisms to others
>
> □ directing credit for success to your people and teammates
>
> □ leading with influence rather than power or control
>
> □ using "guided discovery" rather than direct orders to establish direction

Jerry's "humility in leadership" is the embodiment of leading with reverence. When we follow the principles that he exemplifies, we will change the nature of our organizations. For Jerry, genuinely connecting with the staff is a critical element. Getting close to the work helped him bridge the previous divide. Understanding our staff's both work environment and home pressures will help us lead with our values. The following is a very pointed reminder of the complex lives our staff members live outside the workplace. Regardless of training or position, we need to remember that what seem like major struggles at work may be some of the smallest challenges they have to face. The last part of reverence is honoring the life beyond the workplace.

FAMILY IS A GLASS BALL

The pressure of work can itself be crushing weight in people's lives. If we wish to deeply connect with our staff, then we need to understand the difficulties and struggles they face in their personal lives. Often personal, family struggles can represent the greatest challenges. If we want values-driven leaders and employees, then we must understand that those types of people often hold a deep reverence for family.

Joy writes:

> We had been divorced for about eight years, but these past few years have been particularly difficult.
>
> At the time, we had been in and out of court frequently. There were threats, restraining orders, bullying and demands, and alcoholism that created a constant atmosphere of fear and worry for myself and our son, Tom. Four years earlier, I had thought it was the right thing to do to take a new job offer and relocate to Nashville, so Tom could be close to his father, and I could have some parenting support. But it wasn't working out that way at all.
>
> My cell phone rang; it was Tom. "Mom. Dad's in the hospital. They think he has stomach cancer."
>
> Tom went on to explain how his father, Bill, had been throwing up blood Friday evening, had passed out, and was rushed to the hospital. My ex is a big and strong man—for my son to see him in the hospital looking vulnerable was terrifying for him. In his mind, cancer kills, like it had his grandfather and grandmother just a few years earlier. Was his dad going to die now, too?
>
> The next day, I arrived to Bill's room around noon. His doctor provided me some clarity on his condition. He had a

large orange-sized tumor where his esophagus connected to his stomach, and it had ruptured. They planned to remove the tumor in a couple days. All we could do was pray.

After surgery, the doctor informed me that the tumor was in a tricky place, but they were able to get it all. After further tests, it appeared that Bill had dodged a big bullet—it was a miracle! Bill's cancer had been one of the slowest-growing, least-invasive types of stomach cancers. He wouldn't even need chemo or radiation therapy post-surgery.

By the end of the week, Bill was ready to be released, but we all knew he could not be alone. He needed someone there with him for at least those first few days to make sure he didn't have any issues. Where could he go? Our house was the only suitable answer.

Having Bill in our home was a big deal. Because of all the issues Tom and I had experienced with Bill since our move, we had a family rule. Bill was not allowed in our house unless I was there and had invited him in, and then he was only allowed just inside the door. We needed our safe zone that was "Bill-free." So, for Bill to come to our house to recover, Tom and I needed to be in agreement about that happening and the impact to our home. Reluctantly, we agreed for Bill to move into our upstairs guest room for a week while he healed.

After a week, Bill moved back to his house. Those first few months were hard; every time Bill would come to the house, Tom would retreat to his room. He didn't trust Bill yet and needed to see consistency for lasting proof.

It's been over nine months now since Bill's cancer, and he and Tom have the best relationship they have ever had. It's not perfect, but we all know we want to be together and are working through it with that commitment. Brokenness, whether personal or in a relationship, is an opportunity for you to demonstrate what matters.

My friend Brian Dyson, past CEO of Coca-Cola Enterprises, once told me that we all live our lives juggling multiple balls, from work to family, to interests, to travel, etc. Most of the time, we see these balls all the same, but they're not. Some of these balls bounce when you drop them and things go on fine, with little interruption. But others are made of glass, and these glass balls may or may not recover when you drop them. Family is a glass ball. So, we must never lose focus on its importance in our life. After losing my parents to cancer, going through a painful divorce, and living as a single-mom and full-time executive, the glass ball of family is my most precious. And now, through the miracle of Bill's cancer, we are forming our new family and a glass ball that we are all holding together.

Thank you, God, for this gift of family.

Joy showed amazing tolerance to give her son a chance to develop a relationship with a struggling former spouse. On top of this chaos, the loss of her parents, and the normal struggles of raising a child, she also had career responsibilities. How many of your staff members are juggling family loss, multigenerational responsibilities, relationship disruptions, or a financial crisis on top of all the things we press them to accomplish in the workplace?

If we are to truly rise past common respect and treat our staff with reverence, then we need to embrace and support them—and all that comes with them.

CHAPTER 5 TAKEAWAYS

☐ Living your values requires more than polite respect for others; it requires reverence.

☐ The more special you treat executives, the less special everyone else feels.

☐ Reverence places people over profits, people over egos, people over convenience.

☐ Reverence for others takes humility—but it results in deeper connections, deeper wins, and a greater organization.

☐ The more complicated the lives of our staff, the more they need us to understand those struggles.

CHAPTER 6

COMMUNICATE DEEPLY

Talk to start, listen to connect, and act to cement.

When it comes to communication, there is always some risk involved, but would you risk the livelihood of an organization that had taken you over two decades to build for a cause no one might join? Would you have the courage needed to tell your fellow industry leaders that their practices were actually harming people?

Years after Don Berwick started the Institute for Healthcare Improvement (IHI), he and Maureen Bisognano faced a major test to their values and courage. IHI was healthy and making more progress than any other group in improving quality and lowering the cost of healthcare. The organization relied heavily on the support of hospitals and healthcare providers who attended its conferences, joined its improvement collaboratives, and participated in its training programs.

A dilemma arose when IHI needed to tell these very same organizations that they were injuring hundreds of thousands of patients. In 1999, the Institute of Medicine reported that each year as many as 98,000 patient deaths are related to unintentional medical error: systems errors, insufficient discipline, resistance to change, human error, and other fixable causes.[7]

IHI's leadership wanted to communicate clearly that there was a problem, that their partners in the healthcare sector needed to fix it, and to set a schedule for achieving measurable results. They wanted to set real goals and a firm timetable. Their thinking was summed up this way: "*Some* is not a number, *soon* is not a time."[8]

There is clarity in the notion of not letting *doing* something be confused with *accomplishing* something. There is often a big gap between doing and accomplishing.

Similarly, the answer to "*when?*" cannot be, "*soon.*" Successful organizations frame it in a much more demanding way: *how much by when?* That's a strong business practice used pointedly here to emphasize the great purpose at hand. The value to having this clarity early in the discussion is immense.

Thus began IHI's "100,000 Lives Campaign." The initiative aimed to save a hundred thousand lives that otherwise might be lost in the next eighteen months. At its deepest level, it implied that a hundred thousand people were dying now who could, and should, be saved if healthcare did its work differently. Such a premise could be insulting to the crowd with whom they planned to work. These were the organizations that paid their bills. These were their friends and

---

7   "To Err Is Human: Building a Safer Health System," *Institute of Medicine* (2000), edited by Linda T. Kohn, Janet M. Corrigan, and Molla S. Donaldson.

8   Don Berwick, "Chapter 2: Some Is Not a Number, Soon Is Not a Time," *Promising Care: How We Can Rescue Health Care by Improving It* (San Francisco: Jossey-Bass, 2014).

colleagues. IHI's stance required big courage driven by deep values in the face of the economic realities and political correctness. Their communication said we had an opportunity to save the lives of a hundred thousand people over the next eighteen months if we joined together, shared best practices, and tackled this in a positive way. It had to move beyond courageous; it required a disciplined approach to packaging and implementing the idea. They knew there were risks; they were exposing all the people with whom they were going to work to potentially intense scrutiny and harsh public criticism.

Those joining the effort would have to admit that they were not nearly as good as they could be. They would require the discipline to change and would need to be willing to invest in learning from others.

Despite the obvious challenges, the response was unprecedented. Instead of major angst and pushback, there was huge excitement. Eventually, three thousand of the five thousand hospitals in the United States enrolled. IHI and this program did more to improve care and lower costs over the last two decades than had any other activity in the country. It required clear communication consistent with the driving values, aiming for a big goal in a set time, and the discipline to carry it through.

COURAGE AND CLARITY IN COMMUNICATION

How we communicate is closely tied to what we believe and how we prioritize our time.[9] We will never get that deep respect—deep to the point of reverence—that we aimed for in the previous chapter without great effort to listen and act guided by deep values. However, regardless of the topic, this approach is constantly tested. Financial

---

9   Patterson et. al, *Crucial Conversations: Tools for Talking When Stakes Are High* (McGraw-Hill, 2002).

issues, for example, seem to bring out the best or worst in our departments or organization.

Dwight Klaasen, the professor we met in chapter 3, was asked to lead the planning group that was responsible for all the financial allocations (capital and operations) across all departments at his university. This activity was a common source of tension and distrust in many departments, which often led to political maneuvering. The group had representation from many different sectors of the campus, but most were there to act early and speak loudly to get their favorite, mostly self-serving items approved before the historically difficult negotiations at the end of the process. Unfortunately, this is common in many organizations—a classic case of the Tragedy of the Commons, an economic parable in which individuals attempt to benefit disproportionately from community property, resulting in depleted resources for all.[10] Many of the participants probably taught Tragedy of the Commons in their classes but then behaved in a self-serving way when it came down to the money.

Every one of us in our businesses, schools, faith communities, or civic organizations has experienced the race to grab resources, the disruption it causes, and the angst that persists even after the process has finished. The university was no different, but Dwight wanted to change that. He started by not allowing any early sweetheart approvals, even if they sounded solid. No okays were to be issued until everyone's voice had been heard. This caused some agitation in the group but was heralded by those who felt they had been pushed aside in the past. It sent an important message: no special deals, everyone's voice counts.

---

10   Garrett Hardin, "The Tragedy of the Commons," *Science* 162, no. 3859, http://www.geo.mtu.edu/~asmayer/rural_sustain/governance/Hardin%201968.pdf.

Next Dwight visited every dean and director individually to make sure he understood how their requests served the university's mission and helped to prepare them for the next big step. All of them were invited to present their proposals in person and have a chance to answer questions from those on the commission. The deans felt better heard, more valued, and more confident that those outside their areas who would help decide funding issues were better informed. Regardless of the outcome, the deans felt more involved in the process, felt they had been dealt with more fairly, and were more likely to be supportive of the outcome, even if it was not exactly what they had proposed.

It's always a risk setting up a new plan, but Dwight's focus on a values-driven (rather than politically driven) process with clear communication and transparent goals won the day. Easy? Not at all; it required a ton of time, courage to take on the less-than-happy players, and discipline to stick with his personal principles and those guiding the organization.

Despite being part of all of our daily lives in and out of the workplace, poor communication is a constant deficit in our attempts to build people and organizations. Dwight's story and the others in this chapter will help to illustrate several key principles:

- Strong, clear communication is a great tool to spread consistent values.

- Communication is a dual responsibility: staff needs to seek information and leaders need to provide it in multiple venues and forms.

- Small encounters, clear messages, and personal connections have an additive and ripple effect.

- Imagining that communication occurred is the most frequent error, and using the chain of command as the mainstay to correct that error is a close second.

No attempt to employ honest, bold communication is easy. From the start, as you have may have experienced, there are tough questions and clear risks. Fortunately, most of us are not called upon to communicate our values across a whole country to thousands of organizations, like Don Berwick had to. However, the principles outlined through these stories are applicable to any department or organization.

MAKING IT WORK ON THE FRONT LINE

Books and articles on staff communication and engagement are plentiful and suggest a wide range of strategies. I will try to point out a few that worked very well for us and how they fit in with our plan to build a great place to work that serves a higher purpose.

First, you must define the ground rules. The compact in chapter 5 talked about respect for all. That is clear and constant. Without that mandate and expectation, much of the rest of your work will be inefficient. Another commitment must be to dual responsibility. The information must be provided so it is clear, timely, and consistent, but staff has the responsibility to access the information. "I'm busy," or, "No one told me," can slow progress and create entitlement. In the compact from chapter 5, leaders have a responsibility, but staff is required to engage, as well. You also have to remember that we don't all receive, learn from, or have access to the same forms of media. Our approach was to communicate in three mediums: online, a printed weekly paper, and postings in staff areas. This ensured that all critical information would be available. If we are consistent and clear, it provides an easy path for staff to honor their obligation to be actively informed. Your solutions may be different, but clarity of ground rules and consistent follow-through will establish a foundation for successful communication.

Next, get out of your office, and go to where the work is being done. Lean management system gets a bad rap for being mechanical, but its human connection elements are at the core of its success. *Go and see* is one part of Lean that really provides perspective.[11] Just listening to reports in a meeting doesn't give you the same feeling as visiting the actual people, places, and processes firsthand. The first excuse that many would make for this is that they just don't have the time. Yes, your schedule is full, but full of what? Find time to take your boss and key people from other departments out with you. It will help you to get to know them but, more importantly, it will help your communication. You will be trusted more, you will have noticeably more empathy, and you will understand the work.[12]

It's good to get out to where the work is being done, but going out to different worksites can have very different strategies. Of course, you can't visit everyone, but when you do visit, it won't go unnoticed. Sit down next to a staff member, ask him what he is working on, ask if he has the tools he needs, ask what barriers he experiences, and ask what could be done to help him be more effective or efficient. It will take a little time, but it will be worth it. He will tell those around him, which will help your stated aims of clearly communicating with staff. Furthermore, your communication will be richer, better informed, and better received.

---

11   John Toussaint, *On the Mend: Revolutionizing Healthcare to Save Lives and Transform the Industry* (Lean Enterprise Institute, 2010).

12   Quint Studer, *Hardwiring Excellence: Purpose, Worthwhile Work, Making a Difference* (Fire Starter Publishing, 2003).

Engaging in sit-down department meetings when people have more time to talk, interact, and reflect has great rewards and not only helps to build that culture of reverence you're striving for but also provides you with many lasting insights. These sit-downs should have a different feel and timeframe than an operations worksite visit, but the outcome will be similar. That may require very focused inquiry and flexible interactions.

Give staff a chance to talk about what is important to them. Try holding a mixed staff or all-organization/all-division open forum. You can start with a topic, but the emphasis should be on forum, not lecture. The key to building a great place is trust; it deepens everything, speeds up progress, and enables so much more.[13] Trust will increase if you allow yourself to be more open to what is on their agenda, not just your own. This is about treating their issues with respect, which is not always easy to do.

One day I was in an open meeting with a large group of our staff at a time when the organization was facing some huge ongoing issues: raising our quality, keeping our costs down, adjusting to changing demographics, and upgrading our technologies. Looking forward to a stimulating conversation, early in the forum I opened it up for questions. The first question posed asked, "What about the parking situation?" The complaint was that the staff parking was too far to walk (three hundred yards) and that staff should be able to park in the lots reserved for patients (lots too small to accommodate both staff and patients). Although it would have been easy to dismiss the question and leave it at, "I park three hundred yards away, so can you," holding true to our principles meant listening to staff concerns. I asked what alternatives to parking or transportation they

---

13   Stephen Covey, *The Speed of Trust: The One Thing That Changes Everything* (Free Press, 2008).

had thought of, and I reminded them that our patients would always have priority on parking places. I tried to demonstrate empathy but also clarity on values.

The next question allowed me to show humility. A member of our facilities department asked what I thought the Spanish debt crisis was going to do to our retirement funds. He was sure if Spain defaulted, Italy would go as well, and then other countries would follow. I had the opportunity to point out that it was a fascinating question and then quickly admit I had no idea. I referred him to our CFO to talk through the possibilities.

The information is less important than your willingness to embrace what is important to the group. This makes all your other communications more valuable. Once you have been seen out rounding, listening on their turf in staff meetings, allowing anyone from any department to ask anything of you, and maintaining clear and concise communication, you will notice a change.

Every other week I would send a note to everyone in the organization, titled "Keeping You Informed." This is not so unusual. In fact, it is a standard communication tool. My advantage is that I had had these conversations with the staff, I had seen what went on, and I could highlight who was excelling and where we needed to find a better way forward. This can be scaled up to a larger organization or adapted for small organizations or businesses. This is communication informed by real people that extends way beyond information to culture building.

KEEPING YOU INFORMED

Dear Colleagues,

How far does your impact reach? Making the day better for a patient or colleague is important work; changing the lives of patients, families or colleagues is our great opportunity and responsibility. Often, though, we are unaware of how deeply that extra effort touches another person.

We have great patient experience scores on surveys in the inpatient arena (HCAHPS) and the outpatient practices (CGCAHPS). Those scores are encouraging, but the impact on individuals is really the prize.

Some of you may have seen the story about the first ever Institute for Healthcare Improvement (IHI) conference in San Paulo, Brazil. There, 2,000 people from 25 countries came to learn from each other. The group included six organizations from the United States, and we were one of them. IHI asked me to tell the participants how you take care of patients and the community, how you deliver great quality care while keeping costs down, and how you innovate in clinical care as well as in programs like sustainability and advanced care planning.

The attendees take great heart in the fact that we don't have to be huge like Kaiser Permanente or Cleveland Clinic to deliver great care for patients and the community. I wish you all could have been there to hear how excited they were to learn what you have done and how you have done it.

They are impressed you are aiming for great...and not just okay.

Thanks for your life-changing and now world-changing work!

Sincerely,

Jeff Thompson, MD, *Chief Executive Officer*, Gundersen Health System

We learn best and change from hearing stories that strike a chord within us.

—JOHN P. KOTTER

Finally, strive to balance the perpetual drive to improve and serve better with the celebration of what you have accomplished. Avoid hubris and complacency, but build hope by reveling in the success. How much people need recognition varies from person to person and from department to department. You don't need to sort all that out. You know the values, you know the goals, and you know—regardless of how people are wired—that nearly all will appreciate recognition for real work accomplished.

You must also balance the need to get better faster with the need to let staff know along the way that they are appreciated and that what they do has value. We will talk about driving toward excellence in the next chapter, but there are many ways to acknowledge progress. Remember the rounding? In organizations that have visual progress boards that openly display progress, staff members are able to see and discuss their contributions and any improvements being made. This is of enormous value to the individual, the team, and the organization. It's yet another great opportunity for you to teach and praise.

It's no different in large groups. I recall a department improvement presentation that ended with an apologetic, "We only saved $20,000." In a large organization, it's easy to feel that such an amount would not make a big difference. But as I pointed out, "We have three hundred departments. If they all saved the same amount, we would save $6 million!" If you take those local successes and then have the best presented to an open meeting with leadership in attendance, then you have a chance to make an even bigger deal about their work. It also helps to teach staff about other departments. Cross-organizational learning builds trust, enhances the spread of ideas, and leads to greater collaboration on the next big change.

This constant effort to listen, honor the staff's ideas, and establish a two-way responsibility helps make every day a better work day and helps you celebrate great achievements. Equally important, it establishes a depth of trust and connection to the staff that helps the leaders lead and the organization continue to function when things go poorly. We cannot control everything in the world around us, but the sincerity and consistency of your messages backed up with visible actions will make it much easier for all to thrive, even when times are difficult.

When hard times come, we are often asked to communicate hard messages. We are asked to tell the truth on broad organizational struggles, demonstrate great candor on personnel evaluations, explain painful program changes, or even help staff deal with devastating family or social struggles. Courage to humbly, but firmly, lead with your values can see you through difficult times.

Leading with your values will give you the courage to do what you believe is right, even under pressure. Such is the situation one reporter found himself in while covering a fatal car wreck.

COMMUNICATION PROVIDES CLARITY
IN DIFFICULT SITUATIONS

As a frontline news reporter, Chris Hardie was assigned to cover the police department in La Crosse, Wisconsin. After a tragic car accident that resulted in three deaths, he noticed that the police report contained the name and telephone number of the family member of the departed who had been notified. The question was, should he call her? The story would be shallow and mechanical without an understanding of the victims and their lives. The family might appreciate having a deeper public description of their loved ones. On the other hand, the grieving relative may be angry and insulted that he was prying into the family's lives at a time of great loss.

What would you do? Would you call? You get to choose who might take the beating: if you don't call, the lives of the people who died in the accident will quickly fade into obscurity, the richness that could be shared will be lost to the public, and the grieving relatives may feel worse; or, if you do call, you might take the beating. Chris chose the latter. He decided that it was better he take the lumps than to have the family feel that their loved ones had not been honored.

He called the family member, a woman who had just lost her husband, son, and stepson. She told Chris that the three had been on their way back from a cross-country meet where another son was competing. They did everything together and loved spending time together as a family. Chris thanked her for her time and willingness to share. Then she stopped him and asked, "How did the accident happen? The state patrol won't tell me." Chris told her that one of her sons was driving, crossed the center line in a construction zone, and was struck by another vehicle. "Thank you," she said. "I needed to know."

If Chris can take on such a hard and delicate life-defining moment with courage, candor, and compassion, then we can do the same in our communications with our staff. The focus was not on his ego, but on the greatest good for the most people, especially those who were hurting most deeply.

COMMUNICATE TO UNDERSTAND

Unless we take care of our staff—really take care of our staff—they cannot truly take care of those they are responsible for. Here is a story about how a challenge to deeply communicate and a system that supported communication transcended the routine to deliver on its promise of compassion and excellence.

Pat Conway, MD, radiation oncologist, writes:

Several years ago, while I was sitting in a large lecture hall, Dr. Berwick (IHI) asked the audience members what we wanted from healthcare, then urged us to discuss it with the people around us. After some discussion about quality, safety, and accessible care, he interrupted and asked again: what did we really want from healthcare?

More discussion ensued with most of us just reiterating our original points with more enthusiasm. Yet again, however, we were interrupted, and Dr. Berwick asked us even more emphatically: what do you *really, really* want from healthcare? Again, there was more discussion with even more enthusiasm, but, at least for me, no new ideas.

He then said what he really, really wanted from healthcare was to be able to continue to cross-country ski and treatment that would allow his continued participation in a favored winter sport. His doctors had recommended joint replacement surgery that would have ended this activity. Dr. Berwick personalized the issue, stating that healthcare needs to focus on understanding and addressing the needs of the patient and not just the usual medical dictum.

Following through on that, today I saw my medical recommendations trumped by what a patient really, really wanted. This patient is a thirty-seven-year-old never-smoker who developed an oral tongue cancer. He's had good surgery, good chemotherapy, and good radiation therapy, but his cancer doesn't care. We have used the best we have to try to give him what he needs from healthcare and his cancer doesn't care. It has spread to other parts of his body, now causing complications resulting in hospitalization. Again, despite more cancer therapy these past two weeks, his cancer has progressed.

This Friday before Labor Day will be a day that many of us who have helped care for this man will never forget. He reported coughing up blood, which prompted us to order a CT scan of the chest showing recurrent cancer in the left lung. Per usual Gundersen service, the scan was done that day and he was seen by pulmonary specialists. A bronchoscopy was done early the next week, confirming that the patient's cancer had indeed returned. His fiancée, the person who has been with him, supporting him throughout this year-and-a-half medical odyssey, informed us that they were planning to get married in November and wondered if this should be moved to a closer date. What followed was a true outpouring of compassion and understanding.

This morning while I was reviewing our new cancer treatment plan, or what I thought he wanted from healthcare, the patient's fiancée informed me that what he really, really wanted was to get married today. While that sounds like an easy task, it really, really wasn't. Walking back from the CCU, the head and neck nurse navigator, Bette Roob, and I thought that somehow we needed to try to make this impromptu wedding happen. Easier said than done. I stopped off at the third floor and wandered into administration. Because the request was so out of the ordinary, I was reluctant to even ask for help. Asking wasn't necessary, as one of the VPs, Bryan Erdman, approached me and said it was also his job to help.

"Let's do this," he said—and like that, the train left the station.

So, how hard can it be to get married in a hospital on a Friday afternoon with most of the senior staff gone? Well, it's not so easy when your marriage license is from another state. Our lead attorney, Dan Lilly, figured out that an emergency marriage license could be obtained if the physician provided appropriate documentation. Dr. Mulrennan provided that piece of the puzzle, stating the patient's condition met criteria for an emergency marriage license. Pastoral care got involved and officiated the ceremony. All of the flowers from the gift shop appeared, as did a large, personalized cake from Nutrition Services. Music was played and sung. Photos and videos were taken. A hospital room was even decorated to look like a wedding suite. Staff went all out—ensuring a wedding dinner was arranged. But most importantly, a marriage happened.

I wish I knew all of the people who helped make this happen today. I can't even guess the number. The patient didn't start his new cancer treatment plan today. That had to wait as what he really, really wanted from healthcare today was to be married. We knew this because we were willing to communicate and listen to his needs.

That's stunning care, way outside the normal routine of the day. No CEO said it was okay; no senior VP was asked or involved. The event was sparked by trying to develop deep communication; it was accomplished by staff who knew the values and lived them, moving care from good toward great.

CHAPTER 6 TAKEAWAYS

☐ Establish early on that there is a two-way responsibility when it comes to practicing and honoring your values.

☐ Staff from the front lines and senior executives can and should be participants.

☐ Be courageous to tell the truth in the most-supportive but clearest way possible.

☐ Consistently express your values through actions and words.

☐ Get close enough to the work to enrich your connections and communications.

☐ Be open in rounding, listening, speaking, and writing to gain insight and learn from your staff.

PART III

ORGANIZATION

CHAPTER 7

LEAD TO EXCEED

Have the courage to measure and
improve on excellence.

Excellence sounds great on billboards and mission statements, but how does it look and feel? What are your obligations as a leader? What action are you committed to if excellence is in your values statement?

Suppose you are the manager of a clinic that takes care of breast cancer patients. What goals do you set? What outcomes do you want to achieve? What service will you provide? What are you willing to commit to as you stare into the teary eyes of a patient?

Can you really say the work your people do is "fine" and be okay with that? Can you expect patients to trust you if you do not know your outcomes? Can you honestly say you know your outcomes if you are just recalling the last several patients you happened to see that day? At a time when your patient is scared and most vulnerable, they will not always be in a state to evaluate options in a very complex world of healthcare. It is our responsibility to deliver on what we promise whether they can evaluate us or not.

At Gundersen, we built our breast center by focusing on the experience of the patient. To do so, we took the broadest definition of patient experience. Not just access and ambiance but outcomes and follow-through. Our center was the first to be recognized by the National Quality Measures for Breast Centers Program for excellence. How did a breast center in a medium-sized health system, far from universities and without big philanthropy or government grants, become measurably one of the best in the country? How did we move into the ranks of amazing places like Stanford and Johns Hopkins?

Excellence is to do a common thing in an uncommon way.
—BOOKER T. WASHINGTON

The underpinning value was to treat every patient as if she were a member of our family. The underpinning operational practice was focus on outcomes—all outcomes: social, clinical, short-term, and long-term. It was not based on guessing, but on measuring. Because of a group of people who aimed for excellence, understood how to work together, worked on continuous improvement, and aimed for not just good, but great, outcomes, our breast center was able to achieve excellence.

Did this great initiative have a leader? Of course, it had a strong, values-driven leader: Jeff Landercasper. Quiet, humble, and driven, Jeff was relentless, not for growth or fame, but in delivering on a commitment to the patients.[14] He did it with the help of a broad group of talented people interested in these same principles, a group very close to the work. The group members knew that they were not perfect, but they had the courage to measure.

You can't improve unless you measure it.

—LORD KELVIN

The staff at our breast center was working and continually improving on an already high-functioning structure. And they had a disciplined disregard for conventional wisdom. They refused to accept that only a large university center could be the best. As leaders, we all need to move past the notion of defining greatness on the basis of size, reputation, or marketing budget, and instead expect greatness to be defined by broad outcomes measured across time, demographics, and sectors of the community. Jeff's work became the underpinning of breast care measurement across the US. It wasn't the size of the effort or any department; it was a commitment to one of the key values of excellence.[15]

As mentioned in chapter 6, moving from good toward great will work best if you have a set pattern of open two-way communication, transparency of intent, clear goals and outcomes, improvement tools that engage all staff, and leaders who are close enough to the work to feel the moral imperative to the customers or patients. This is

---

14   Jim Collins, "Level 5 Leadership: The Triumph of Humility and Fierce Resolve," *Harvard Business Review*, July–August, 2005, https://hbr.org/2005/07/level-5-leadership-the-triumph-of-humility-and-fierce-resolve.

15   Landercasper et. al, "A Community Breast Center Report Card Determined by Participation in the National Quality Measures for Breast Centers Program," *Breast Journal* 16, no. 5 (2010): 472–480.

another opportunity to teach your leaders to be responsible for their staff's success (looking forward) rather than holding them accountable (looking backward).

The breast center used these tools and the approach outlined in previous chapters to excel. This work is set within an organization that has a clear and present Strategic Plan, unwavering values, and the courage and discipline to follow through. Below is our one-page Strategic Plan. From the first day of orientation, this was integrated into our staff, departments, and board functions. We were consistent on where we were going, the prominence of the values, and the connectedness of all the strategies to serve the mission and accomplish the purpose. Clarity of direction gave departments, like the breast center, the freedom to design a strong path forward.

GUNDERSEN
HEALTH SYSTEM® STRATEGIC PLAN

*Our Purpose is to bring health and well-being
to our patients and communities.*

Mission: We will distinguish ourselves through excellence in patient care, education, research and improved health in the communities we serve.

Vision: We will be a Health System of excellence, nationally recognized for improving the health and well-being of our patients, families, and their communities.

Commitment: We will deliver high quality care because lives depend on it, service as through the patient were a loved one, and relentless improvement because our future depends on it.

Values: **Integrity** – Perform with honesty, responsibility and transparency.

Excellence – Measure and achieve excellence in all aspects of delivering healthcare.

Respect – Treat patients, families, and coworkers with dignity.

Innovation – Embrace change and contribute new ideas.

Compassion – Provide compassionate care to patients and families.

Superior Quality and Safety
Demonstrate superior Quality & Safety through the eyes of the patients & caregivers.

Outstanding Patient Experience
Create an outstanding Experience for patients and families.

Great Place
Create a Culture that embraces a passion for caring and a spirit of improvement.

Affordability
Make our care more Affordable to our patients, employers, and community.

Growth
Achieve Growth that supports our mission and other key strategies.

MEASURING OUTCOMES, CHALLENGING LEADERSHIP

Every idea requires a good plan. But ultimately, plans don't count. Outcomes count. A strategic plan is just a tool, a great tool—an important tool for communication and guidance—but just a tool. The outcomes were promised through our values and mission. At Gundersen, we delivered on that promise.

The Commonwealth Fund recognized our organization as one of the sixteen best systems in the country, and Healthgrades voted us one of the fifty best hospitals in the country for outcomes.[16] For ten years in a row we ranked in the top 5 percent in the nation in outcomes.[17] Our outpatient service level went from the twenty-fifth to ninetieth percentile. In a town of fifty-five thousand, we had twenty-five thousand job applicants in one year. Our information technology services stayed ahead of or on par with anyone else's. We kept our pledge to lower our fee increase each year, a feat we honored

16   The Commonwealth Fund, www.commonwealthfund.org.

17   Healthgrades, www.healthgrades.com.

for sixteen years in a row, despite charging seniors so little for their care that we are in the first percentile for Medicare spending in the last two years of life. We were far from perfect, but our image in the community shifted from that of a business to one of community partner.

We didn't get there by accepting disappointing outcomes. We got there by comparing ourselves to the ideal and striving for greatness. Everyone must be responsible for serving the higher goals, but especially leadership. In far too many organizations, "good enough" is accepted as the best they can do. It takes courage to admit that you are not on par with the ideal and take action to make positive changes.

In 2002, John Toussaint, MD, was the CEO of ThedaCare, a community health system headquartered in Appleton, Wisconsin.[18] He was frustrated with the billboard claims of excellence, the underlying poor performance, and slow improvement of healthcare organizations. He called several of his counterparts from around the state, I among them, to help form a plan to open the discussion and drive improvement more quickly. Together, the five collaborating healthcare CEOs concluded that if we could agree to employ a single approach to measure outcomes, it would give us stronger comparisons and better arguments for improvement to use with our own staff, and even drive our competitors to improve. We also had an obligation to patients, families, and employers to live closer to our mission statements. No secrets, no special club—this was about the health and well-being of the statewide community. We formed the Wisconsin Collaborative for Healthcare Quality.[19] Within the first year, it became open for anyone to join; anyone could learn from the

18 John Toussaint, *Potent Medicine: The Collaborative Cure for Healthcare* (ThedaCare Center for Healthcare Value, 2012).

19 Wisconsin Collaborative for Healthcare Quality, www.wchq.org.

others. You only had to be willing to report your progress openly and work on improving. We were self-imposing a level of discipline that few had at the time. We were going to measure against the best of each of us and make the findings public.

Comparing yourself to your mediocre past, or mediocre peers, is not excellence.

When the first public report came out one year later, we looked pretty weak. Our performance compared with the rest of the country turned out to be good, but compared with our potential—to the ideal—we were an embarrassment. Much to our surprise, the 250 business leaders who had gathered to hear this first-of-its-kind report were grateful, appreciative, and complimentary of our candor. They had not before seen such transparency, did not know we had made such progress in one year, and wanted to know what they could do to help. They were not surprised by the mediocre results: they and their staff were living them. Once measuring and reporting became more open around the country, the results stood up very well compared with others, but, as noted earlier, that was a weak bar; compared to where we wanted to be, we had much work to do. Our values said *integrity*; to claim we were great was not true. Our values said *excellence*; to be better than mediocre is not excellent. The risk of admitting we were not as good as we needed to be was outweighed by our desire to act true to our values. To move toward excellence, we needed to admit we were not yet there, measured against the best, and proceed to improve on those outcomes. Zero defects or 100 percent reliability might not be possible, but you don't know until you make that your goal.

Excellence driven by a moral imperative at the individual level (like the breast center) or partnerships across organizations and geography (like the collaborative) are either enhanced or made vulnerable by one key element: people. More specifically, leadership. A leader's approach and actions will either cast an illuminating, invigorating light or a disruptive depressing shadow. When we as leaders get something right, people are amazed and inspired by the progress. But when we get something wrong, its effect is multiplied far more than mistakes made on the front lines. Here are a few diagrams to help explain.

A normal organizational chart shows lines depicting who is responsible for whom. The CEO is responsible for the whole organization, while the frontline staff is mostly responsible for themselves.

LINES OF RESPONSIBILITY

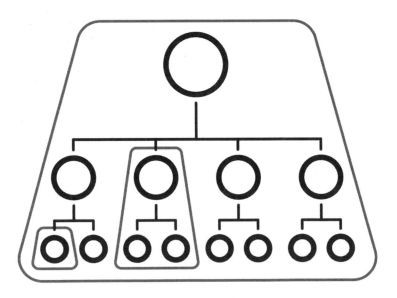

Looks clean but this is not how things really work.

LINES OF INFLUENCE

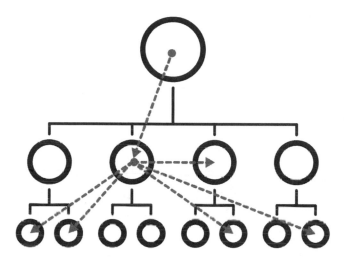

If we look at lines of influence, we see that they are not as crisp and will not follow a set pattern. In addition, lines of influence shift and change with time. Most importantly, it shows that a high performer or a disruptive troublemaker in leadership casts a large shadow. The higher up in the organization a leader is, the broader influence they yield, good or bad. This is not news to most of us, yet there is a great deal of literature and personal experience that points to a slow or minimal response to low performance and bad behavior in the upper ranks. Clearly, the impact on quality and morale is greater when leadership falls short. Yet, so often, it is allowed to persist and issues are not addressed. We saw a great illustration of this in chapter 4 with the two senior leaders and their influence outside their direct areas of responsibility.

LINES OF IMPACT

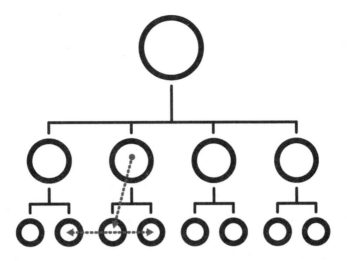

Another important observation is that desire and actions leading to superior performance affect those beside, above, and below you on the chart. Although the impact of the senior members may be greater, even the most-frontline staff can have a significant influence on achieving superior performances through their effect on those around and above them. There are different effects on different staff, but whether the individual is striving for excellence or accepting mediocrity will affect a myriad of those touched.

COURAGE TO PRESS FOR EXCELLENCE

None of this can be done without a dependable team. None of this can be done without a baseline culture that aims for excellence. We are not all lucky enough to work in a department or organization with such a culture. When the system does not support you, it requires individual courage and durability to withstand the struggle and endure the consequences.

The following cases are from Linda Haddad. Linda is an experienced healthcare lawyer, educator, and guide for organizations trying to get better.

Linda writes:

I frequently saw great courage when we engaged in difficult medical staff issues. While the culture has changed a lot over the years, in the early years of my practice there was great pressure to See No Evil. Problem physicians were able to practice for a very long time before anyone would raise a question about the quality of care they provided. The cost of speaking up was too high professionally.

I am reminded of two very brave doctors I was honored to work with. Both were relatively young. I can't share their names or hospitals, but I believe the examples are very valuable.

The first was an orthopedic surgeon, on staff for a few years, who was attracted to the community because of the reputation of the chair of the department. As he watched to learn from the chair, he became confused. He observed care that was not current. He wondered if some of the practices he observed from this surgeon were ever best practices, much less meeting the standard of care. He gingerly asked the surgeon about some of his choices and, at first, was met with an avuncular response that indicated obliquely that the young surgeon had a lot to learn. The more he watched, though, the more he worried.

He finally reported a few specific patient care episodes to the peer review committee that, to their credit, took it seriously. They began a careful review involving the surgeon in question and never revealed the name of the young orthopedist who had brought the information forward.

A couple weeks after the peer review began, the young surgeon attended a meeting of his state's orthopedic society. Lunch was served cafeteria style. When our hero got his tray and went to sit with a table of colleagues, all four got up, took their trays, and moved. Derisive comments from a couple others nearby made it clear that he was not welcome. Nevertheless, he followed through with his concerns and the senior physician soon took emeritus status and was highly regaled at a med staff party but was no longer putting patients at risk. The young surgeon paid a cost, but in the end, ensured that patients would receive better care.

The second was also a rather young specialist who was very distressed by the surgery he observed from the department chair. Cases that should take a few hours took twelve, fifteen, or even twenty-four hours! His reports were incredible. The anesthesiologists were exhausted working with this surgeon and feared for patients anesthetized for so long. This young doctor also had support from his medical staff and a careful review resulted in efforts to get the senior doctor to resign or limit his practice. He vigorously declined. That led to the Medical Executive Committee ultimately recommending revocation of his clinical privileges and proceeded to a hearing.

The president and two former presidents of the national professional society came to the hearing to testify on behalf of their friend, the senior surgeon. They ridiculed the "overconfident and undereducated" complainant. The young surgeon realized he had no political future in the profession but has continued to work successfully in the hospital.

Unfortunately, Linda's experience is common in many organizations, not just healthcare. We have made progress, but the theme of special privileges for the well connected is universal. In Linda's examples, the key to breaking it was having individuals with the courage to speak up, backed by organizations guided by values and organized to serve the greater good, not individuals.

No one's ego should be more important than the well-being of a patient, student, or a community.

SETTING THE BAR FOR EXCELLENCE

Perhaps you already spend considerable energy measuring and comparing your company or organization's outcomes. Maybe you compare to others around you who seem to be doing fine, but *"fine"* probably isn't in your organization's goals. Most organizational goals prescribe superior performance, a "best in class" standard of excellence.

Jim Reinertsen, MD, was a senior improvement fellow at IHI. Although few healthcare systems actually measured against the best, Reinertsen knew that most had committed, at least verbally, to excellence, or to being the best in their class. He stated bluntly, if you measure only against your peers, you could be the best in that group, but that means you may very well have risen to be the "cream of the crap." If your goal is greatness, but you are only better than other mediocre performers, then you are still a long way from great. Accomplishing less than our true potential is a waste. Comparing against the best possible, aiming for the ideal, and proving you are providing the most benefit for the most people, is what moves organizations from good to great.

CHAPTER 7 TAKEAWAYS

☐   To live our values, our goals must be bolder than mediocrity.

☐   Hope is a weak strategy for improvement. Staff will be inspired by big, bold goals aimed at the well-being of others.

☐   No one's ego is more important than consistently living the values.

☐   Measure, don't guess. Use common tools that build, not limit.

☐   Embed the values into every orientation, communication, evaluation, and goal.

☐   Have the discipline to build and use a system that supports those that live the values.

☐   "Holding accountable" is looking backward. "Being responsible for their success" is looking forward. Excellence will be found in the balance.

CHAPTER 8

INNOVATE TO SERVE VALUES

Have a disciplined disregard for conventional wisdom.

Decisions involved in end-of-life care are among the most challenging aspects of healthcare. This is something patients, their families, and their doctors must decide, with emphasis on compassion and dignity. Unfortunately, all too often the patient's wishes are unknown and well-intentioned family members can have very different ideas regarding what they would want.

Imagine being an emergency department nurse and finding yourself in the middle of such a dispute. Imagine having to decide the best course for the patient while members of their family fiercely advocate for different approaches. A son wants to spare no expense or effort to save his mother; a daughter believes the best thing to do is to make her comfortable. The patient's wishes are unknown; what would you do?

This is the situation that unfolded a number of years ago concerning a lovely eighty-two-year-old woman named Mabel. She had been a long-time dialysis patient who had just suffered a debilitating stroke that threatened to end her life. Mabel's daughter, who had cared for her for some time, was at her bedside. She had spent a lot of time with her mom, and she didn't think that she would want aggressive support. "Let's just keep her comfortable," she suggested.

Mabel's son was a nice man, but he hadn't talked with his mom about important issues for several years. He had different ideas. He argued, "I know she is tough. I know she would want us to do everything, so I think we should send her to the ICU and put her on a ventilator. I am sure she will get better; she's a fighter!"

Now, we all die. Trust me, I am a doctor and I know something about death. I know all of us reading this are a little closer to that event than we were yesterday. The big question is not if we are going to die but how are we going to live up to that moment? And who will make decisions regarding our quality of life?

As Mabel gasped for air and began to turn dusky, the disagreement between the two siblings escalated. Imagine being the nurse in the middle of this delicate but critical dispute. What would you do? This is a life-and-death situation for Mabel, but you have no idea what she wants. The implications for both the family and the staff are enormous and long lasting.

Sadly, situations like this were common. So, many times we would find ourselves saying, "If only we knew what the patient wanted." To better know what Mabel and the many patients in similar straits would have wanted, we needed to get closer to the patient and closer to our core values.

The mission of our health system is to improve the health and well-being of patients and the communities we serve. Our values include compassion, respect, and excellence. Our inability to respect the wishes of patients like Mabel was not consistent with that mission or those values.

To address these critical decisions, Bud Hammes, PhD, Gundersen's clinical ethicist, led a patient-focused, system-supported approach that would better serve our mission and values. He and the clinical staff had been at many bedsides and had many difficult discussions. It was clear we needed a better plan that would include other healthcare providers, the faith community, and many interested civic groups.

We needed a plan that would clearly explain to patients what their options might be in various health situations, a plan that would allow them to define their wishes and foster communication with them *before* they were desperately ill. Patients needed to understand their options in the event of traumatic injury or at different points along a disease trajectory—from aggressive care to comfort care only—and to know that their wishes would be honored, even when they are no longer able to communicate for themselves.

Plenty of mistakes were made by us and the rest of the medical field in trying to address this issue. Simply filling out a form or telling the health professionals that they should talk to patients about these matters did not work. What it took was an innovation by people close to the work, a system to support the design, and the courage to ignore the common thinking of the day: that these matters could not and should not be led by healthcare.

It has been well argued that clinicians should be at the center of this plan.[20] We believed that clinicians were critical to initiating the discussion, but it was equally important to have well-trained staff, such as nurses and social workers, equipped with a structured, documented approach with consistent language and definitions, across the community as a whole.

The health delivery system had to be clear that the wishes of the patients were paramount—that not following the patient's wishes was a cause for peer review, no different from a medication or surgical error. And there needed to be a process to measure those activities. Inspired by staff close to the work, we established a structure that allowed the patient's wishes to be known, understood, and updated over time—a structure that spread to competing healthcare organizations, faith communities, and all sections of diverse social groups.

A strong validation of this plan came in 2014. The National Institute of Medicine report on the key elements of advance care planning stated that when it came to end of life care, healthcare facilities should have (1) an electronic health record, (2) physician orders for life-sustaining treatment, and (3) a system of care best represented by that developed at Gundersen. We didn't accept the situation as it was; we raised the bar and set a new standard.[21]

The plan sounds straightforward but is quite difficult. At the time, electronic health records were either not available or not set up to document these repeated conversations. Outpatient staff who thought they were doing fine had to change—some had to be inspired, urged, or nudged to include this as part of their total

---

20   Atul Gawande, *Being Mortal: Medicine and What Matters in the End* (Picador, 2015).

21   National Institute of Medicine, "Dying in America: Improving Quality and Honoring Individual Preferences Near the End of Life," *National Institute of Medicine*, 2014.

scope of care, and each community had myriad ideas that needed to be listened to and honored. On the national front, you had to be durable enough to overcome self-serving opportunists declaring that this work was a "government takeover" of healthcare with the establishment of "death panels." It was a messy process but one that was critical to the plan's success.

And the success was stunning. In 1998, results of a research study about advance care planning in our community were published.[22] Researchers found that over 95 percent of our seniors in the last two years of life had advance care plans available in their medical records, and these plans were followed over 98 percent of the time. That number is way beyond national performance levels. In 2010, results of a similar study were published indicating that those same levels of patient-centered care had been sustained over the decade.[23] Our regional patient satisfaction measures for seniors are some of the highest in the country. These patients are extremely happy with their self-directed care. Our role is to give them the opportunity to choose a system that honors their choices. Interestingly, when they do choose, patients most often choose less-aggressive care. An additional result is that combined with our integrated system focused on quality, this program reduced the government's spending markedly. When it comes to Medicare dollars per capita in the last two years of life, we are in the first percentile. We've achieved distinction—not by rules, but by patient choice.

---

22   B.J. Hammes and B.L. Rooney, "Death and end-of-life planning in one Midwestern community," *Archives of Internal Medicine* no 158, 4 (1998): 383–90.

23   B.J. Hammes, B.L. Rooney, and J.D. Gundrum, "A comparative, retrospective, observational study of the prevalence, availability, and specificity of advance care plans in a county that implemented an advance care planning microsystem." *Journal of the American Geriatrics Society* no 57, 7 (2010): 1249–55.

Critics have attributed our success to a healthy population of retired, bachelor, Norwegian farmers in Wisconsin. However, when you look at the Medicare data via the Dartmouth Atlas and compare it with similar Medicare groups in Los Angeles, Philadelphia, or Miami, our patients are older, poorer, more obese, drink more, and smoke more.[24] Our demographic is not healthier; rather, our approach to patients and the system we developed to support them is healthier.

We have been frequently challenged by senior administrators and financial experts for "leaving so much money on the table." When compared with the average Medicare spending, that money left on the table amounted to tens of millions of dollars every year for twenty years—money we could have claimed if we hadn't been concerned with giving our patients options. We are well aware of the financial impact, but treating seniors in this way is more consistent with our values than trying to balance budgets on seniors' backs with unneeded and unwanted care. That assertion usually shortens the discussion.

Now let's go back to our patient, Mabel. Imagine how much easier it would have been for her family and her if the advance care planning system we have now had been in place. What did happen, and what still happens in many situations like this, is that by using moderate, noninvasive intervention, we bought enough time for an effort by our ethics group, social services, chaplaincy, and clinical staff to have multiple family discussions and chart a course of aggressive palliative care that delivered comfort, pain relief, broad communication, and a focus on the family's needs. It was a good outcome, thankfully, of a difficult situation. Now, with a well-scripted, patient-

---

24   The Dartmouth Atlas of Health Care, www.dartmouthatlas.org.

directed plan, such situations are almost always less of a struggle for patients, families, and staff.

From the patients' perspective, this level of planning, support, and care results in higher quality, lower cost, and greater control over their healthcare than they've ever had. From the staff's perspective, this approach decreases stress and allows them to deeply connect with their patients and families. In order to honor its values, the system had to assume the responsibility for delivering superior care beyond its walls—it had to change its practices and innovate to develop a completely new model to replace the old model that had failed Mabel. The new model had to ensure multiple conversations, organized education, strong community connectedness, a consistent approach to measurement and improvement, and, most importantly, a relentless desire to let patients decide how they wanted to live.

That is one focused example of how people close to the work built a structure to take on an issue that was pervasive but rarely managed well. It took a complex effort that included consistent language, training, and infrastructure to promote innovation. To do so required us to ignore the conventional wisdom that you cannot connect healthcare, work with the government, work with seniors, work with all faiths in a community, or build a model that can work across diverse settings. The outcomes noted are stunning, but it is hard to measure the deeper effects of the comfort of control. You cannot quantify the peace of mind that comes from knowing that your care will be what you want. There is great advantage to having whole communities agree on a way forward, to the benefit of all.

These opportunities—which, if we are to follow our values, are actually obligations—are all around. The following section will suggest three major approaches to improve your chances of taking observations or opportunities and turning them into innovations.

We can find them by watching, listening, and asking questions that go beyond the superficial. Many use the Lean tool of asking "why" five times on a single topic to force yourself to dig deeper, understand more broadly, and engage with others more sincerely.

SUGGESTION 1: GET CLOSE ENOUGH TO THE WORK TO FEEL THE MORAL IMPERATIVE

Let's take a walk, and I will give a couple examples of what seeing more deeply looks like. Although we are going to focus on healthcare, the lessons are applicable to other fields, as well. I think examining successes and failures in other disciplines is always a great way to stimulate innovation in your own area.

My first suggestion on how to innovate more quickly is applicable whether you are a frontline person or in management. The moral imperative might be the human impact of the service (healthcare, education, etc.), the workplace's impact on your staff, or a product's impact on society (fresh water, safe food, or reliable equipment or technology).

As we walk down the hall of a bright, sunlit hospital corridor, we first notice that most staff, visitors, and even patients will have one or more smartphones or tablets. One of the key drivers of that digital, connected revolution was Steve Jobs. He was famous for touching, testing, and going to the design lab to evaluate his next best model. He didn't stay isolated or sheltered from the details. He ignored the conventional wisdom that "CEOs should stay at 30,000 feet." He engaged so he could ask, understand, and guide.

As we continue down the hallway, we come to the pediatric ICU. We meet Dr. Strauss and an outstanding group of dedicated staff. The first patient is a four-year-old boy on a ventilator. He has severe asthma. He struggles for every breath. A good start as a leader, director, or CEO would be to ask whether we are managing the ventilator consistent with best practices. Do we have safety systems for managing the boy's medications? Do we have infection control measures in place to limit, using the best of known science, his chance of acquiring an illness in the hospital? All of those practices and safeguards are needed. But if I'm really close to the work, I would talk with the boy's family and ask about him outside this room. I also would ask, why is he here, or why is he here again? What else is going on that we could change that would affect his whole life, not just during his time in our care?

Now let's continue down the hallway to Dr. Kuffel and her dedicated team in labor and delivery. This will be easier to relate to, since I know that each of you reading this were babies at one time. Here we need to talk about post-delivery bleeding, preventing infections, safety of the staff, and making system changes to eliminate medication errors—all of which are important and part of a high-quality obstetrical service. But if we are really going to get close to the work, we would also ask, how is the baby affected during the pregnancy by things going on with and around the mother? For example, do we ask how many chemicals are found in this baby's blood at the moment it is born? Where did they come from? What harm do they do to the mom or baby? The average number is around one hundred nonhuman chemicals. Some studies have found as few as fifty, others as many as two hundred, but never zero.[25] The question to then ask is, do we have any responsibility for that and, if so, are we going to live our values and take action? We will come back to that soon.

---

25   Sara Goodman, "Tests Find More Than 200 Chemicals in Newborn Umbilical Cord Blood," *Scientific American,* December 2, 2009, www.scientificamerican.com/article/newborn-babies-chemicals-exposure-bpa/.

Continuing our walk, we pass by the adult ICU and the emergency department. Having touched on them earlier in our advance care planning section, we will move on to the clinic. For our purposes, we will focus on a clinic in Boston. Patients are coming and going as you would expect in a busy clinic, but the patients are being observed by a young pre-law student concerned not at all about the high-quality care they were receiving, but rather, with what happens next. She notices a patient coming out with a new prescription for insulin and a nutrition pamphlet about the food she needs to eat. Both had been explained well, but nobody asked whether she has money to buy the insulin. And even if she has money for the insulin, does she have a refrigerator? And if she has a refrigerator, does she have money for electricity to keep it running? And can she afford or does she have access to the food she needs to eat?

Rebecca Onie was the law student who not only asked these questions but who also eventually built a corps of over a thousand student volunteers to ask those questions and work on connecting patients to services that could help meet their medical and social needs. This is getting close to the work—close enough to feel the imperative of the change that must be made.[26] Rebecca could have read about all these issues online in journals and blogs, but she got close to the work and asked questions that led to actionable innovations. For this and many other reasons, many management systems make rounding where the work is done a daily part of a leader's standard expectations.

Finally, if you are still unconvinced and believe I am only speaking about frontline managers, consider Melinda Gates. Despite the ability to stay far away and still make enormous impact with her

---

26   Health Leads, https://healthleadsusa.org/location/boston/.

insight and philanthropy, she chooses to walk through the villages, sit in the huts, hold the people, and get close to her work.[27]

BREAKING THE MOLD

Yesterday's innovation is often today's standard. The things we accept as common place, in many instances, had to break existing molds before they could set the new standard. Today, grocery store chains are common, but that was not always the case. This is the story of Dave and Barb Skogen, the married couple who shattered the mold, going against Dave's father and conventional wisdom to establish a chain of twenty-five grocery stores. Today, their company provides jobs and great service to a wide range of communities.

Dave writes:

In the early 1970s, I was managing the meat department inside my father's small, neighborhood "supermarket." At the time, there were fifty-seven other small, independently operated stores like my dad's in La Crosse. On Wednesday afternoons, when I was off from work, I would grab a local newspaper to see if one or more were for sale, then scout out any that were. Of course, then I would have to convince Dad that we needed to grow.

Dad was old school; everything he bought he paid for with cash. There was simply no way he was ever going to support his sons borrowing money to buy a second store, regardless of how promising the investment was.

"David, this store your mom and I own, is all the store you will ever need to be successful," he once told me.

---

27 "Melinda Gates on what faith in action means to her," World Vision, updated November 3, 2016, www.worldvision.org/girls-and-women-news-stories/melinda-gates-interview.

It was an enjoyable experience scouting potential locations, but the odds were stacked against me.

In 1974, things changed in my favor—growth found me. A local developer was building a strip mall a mile nearby. The developer, Mr. Raymond, was adamant that one of the mall's anchors would be a large supermarket, three times the size of Dad's store, and he wanted the Skogen family to run it. I brought the opportunity to my father and tried to convince him that this new store was a good fit for us. I also told him that if we didn't seize this opportunity, another grocer would. Dad declined, much to my brother's and my disappointment.

We both had tremendous respect for my father and what he had built, but we decided this was too great an opportunity to pass up. With the backing of our wholesaler, we decided to move forward. Soon after construction on our new location began, we received a call from a local competitor who was interested in selling to us. In a flash, we had gone from one small store to a chain with three locations.

As twenty-year-olds, we had no idea what we were in for. But we laced up our shoes and made it work. Today, we are the owners of twenty-five supermarkets. Dad would be so proud to know of our success, and to see our stores serving communities across Wisconsin, providing food, offering work experience in a values-driven organization, and serving as active partners in building communities.

Dave demonstrated a willingness to innovate. Along with his wife, Barb, he took risks, worked hard, and generously gave back to communities. They have accomplished their goals and in doing so have improved the health and well-being of the areas they serve. But to get there, they had to ignore conventional wisdom and the advice of Dave's well-respected father.

The lesson here is to not let anything deter you when you know you have a good idea. Innovation takes courage and a willingness to push past the naysayers—even if they are caring, well-meaning naysayers.

SUGGESTION 2: STRUCTURE IMPROVES INNOVATION

Adding and improving structure will increase the depth of innovation. Let's go back to the tech world for a minute. Do you think that the iPhone is an innovation? I would argue that it is not. I would argue that it is many innovations—dozens, maybe hundreds of innovations. You think it was built by Steve Jobs himself? Or seven geeks in his basement or garage? Of course not. It was built by broad teams with wide-ranging skill sets. It required many teams across many disciplines developing many innovations to ultimately build a great product. How do you get everyone headed in the same direction, free enough to create but focused enough to drive to a breakthrough product or needed improvement?

It is easy to lay out but hard to stay with. Build a plan, aim for goals bigger than an individual, insist on a shared value set, develop a culture of respect, use a staff-engaging system of improvement, and train your leaders to serve not rule.

Good leaders don't tell people what to do; they give teams capability and inspiration.

—JEFFREY IMMELT

Remember our Strategic Plan at Gundersen? It is a clear, one-page outline of where we are going, what is important, and what success is going to look like. Builders, creators, and innovators want to know what they are driving to and why that matters. Be sure to establish clear values that are lived by all—not just by those at orientation, not just by the lower paid staff—but everyone, all the time. To be clear on how the values are lived, codify them in day-to-day language and use the resulting document, your compact, in recruiting, evaluations, and frequent communication. Staff will be more creative and better problem solvers if they are not worrying about how they will be treated. Make sure your improvement tools and process are built for staff engagement, as mentioned in chapters 5 and 7. We have described several of the useful tools that we used to tap into the great experience and creativity of staff who are close to the work. No matter what field you work in, these tools and approaches can be applied to improve quality and encourage innovation.

To make this work, you must ensure that you and your colleagues in leadership have adequate training. You will need to understand the function of your structure and tools, but, most importantly, understand that your job is to use your organization's shared values to build people as they accomplish the organization's goals.

You want to invite new ideas, not new rules.

—DAN HEATH

If all that is done is watchdogging the rules to "hold people accountable," then you will spend much of your time looking backward. Being responsible for individuals' success means looking forward, and doing so will give them the structure and freedom to truly innovate. They will know where you are going, the shared values, and the common tools to invigorate them and enhance their work with their colleagues.

Be close enough to the work to feel its importance, and give staff the kind of structure that allows them to create.

SUGGESTION 3: HAVE A DISCIPLINED DISREGARD FOR CONVENTIONAL WISDOM

Innovation does not come from conventional wisdom. Do not toss everything out the window, but take inventory of and carefully think through your assumptions and your responsibilities to see whether they hold up to the science and your mission statement. Remember the boy in the pediatric ICU? We asked many technical questions, but did we ask why he has asthma? What is our responsibility here? Is it just to fix him up and wait for him to get sick again? Is that the best we can do? Is our only responsibility to wait until he gets desperately ill again?

We did not think that our purpose statement[28] about serving the "health and well-being of patients and the community" meant sitting and waiting. Six million children in the United States have asthma.[29] It is the number-one reason for school absenteeism, which is the last thing kids anywhere, but especially those in poverty, can afford. Even more importantly, thousands of adults and children in the United States die each year of asthma. Around the world, more than six million people die from issues related to indoor or outdoor air pollution every year.[30] Is that our responsibility? Conventional

---

28 Roy Spence Jr., *It's Not What You Sell, It's What You Stand For: Why Every Extraordinary Business is Driven by Purpose* (Portfolio, 2009).

29 "Asthma in the US," CDC, May 2011, www.cdc.gov/vitalsigns/asthma/.

30 "7 million premature deaths annually linked to air pollution," World Health Organization, March 25, 2014, www.who.int/mediacentre/news/releases/2014/air-pollution/en/#content.

wisdom and practices imply that it is someone else's problem to solve. We didn't think so.

Jim Collins would say you have to face the brutal facts. What was our contribution to breathing problems for our patients with asthma, heart disease, or chronic lung disease?[31] In 2008, our use of electricity via a regional coal power plant and heat via natural gas were putting 430,000 pounds of particulate matter per year into the air, air that our asthma patients, heart patients, and chronic lung disease patients were forced to breathe. That was a big problem. Conventional wisdom may say it was somebody else's issue, but we said it was our issue—living our values demanded it. Healthcare is two-and-a-half times more energy intensive than other businesses. Across the country, we are nearly 20 percent of the economy. We put a lot of bad stuff in the air. It hurts patients. Those are the brutal facts.

We decided to break the mold, live our values, and take on the responsibility. When it came to finding a solution, we again had to ignore the conventional wisdom of the day, which says a choice must be made either between jobs and the environment, or between cost savings and the environment. We didn't believe either was true.

Our plan was to decrease our negative impact on the health of our communities, decrease our cost of care, and improve the local economy. "Stick to our core" was an internal argument against this path. Some believed that we had done well with treating sick patients, so we should just wait until people are sick and let someone else solve the community issues. We didn't believe that, either.

Taking on this issue with those parameters of health and economic success drove many innovations. By implementing energy-saving measures and using alternative sources of energy, Gundersen

31   Jim Collins, *Good to Great: Why Some Companies Make the Leap ... and Others Don't* (HarperBusiness, 2011).

reduced our asthma-aggravating particulate matter by over 90 percent, decreased the cost of care, and helped to boost local economy. Details of this amazing success will be elaborated on in chapter 11.

In 2015, the world's nations and Fortune 500 companies convened in Paris and promised reductions in particulate matter emissions of 30 to 50 percent over the next several decades. Gundersen's results were presented there, showing a 91 percent decrease in greenhouse gases in just eight years. That was a remarkable accomplishment for our efforts. All the better, we saved money and improved the local economy at the same time.

That's a story about great success, but that's only the beginning. Let's go back to labor and delivery. Remember that mother and her baby? Remember the one hundred chemicals that were in the baby's blood when it was born? That is our problem, too. Do you think we were responsible for any of the contaminants in the environment that end up in babies' blood streams? Whether we liked it or not, we had to admit that we were.

The key to addressing this issue was, once again, getting close to the work. We had our staff get close to the sewer treatment workers, the Environmental Protection Agency, and the Department of Natural Resources. As we discussed earlier, medicine or chemicals that are put down the drain don't just go away. Chemicals and many pharmaceuticals survive the sewage treatment system and re-emerge in our air and water. "Flush it away and make it someone else's problem" has been a commonly accepted practice with serious ramifications. We decided to fix that, as well. We will go into detail later, but we accomplished our goal—our hazardous pharmaceutical waste is down 2,000 percent, and we save more than $10,000 each month in the process. Again, this required courage to take on the problem, discipline to make a solution work, and durability to put up with the criticism and hard work of breaking new ground.

Another issue was the National Child Protection Training Center, which we talked about in chapter 2. Some believed that the center was not central to our work and that it was too risky a venture. Conventional wisdom would have said, "Let someone else take that on. The risks that accompany being associated with child abuse cases or with sexual abuse education and prevention are just too high." But we said that the center's mission was consistent with our own, so we figured out a way to make it serve our communities, make it financially viable, and allow it to continue to teach child protection to tens of thousands of professionals in healthcare, education, law enforcement, and social services across the country.

In chapter 7, we talked about our breast center. Ours was the first breast center in the country to be a center of excellence—so designated not by magazines, but by the breast centers themselves. This recognition was because of such strong outcomes—outcomes made possible because everyone, including the leaders, were close to the work, and because smart, caring people worked within a structure that ensured they knew where they were going and how they were going to get there. This allowed them to innovate more quickly and perform more consistently. And finally, any conventional wisdom about leaving greatness to the large, famous centers was ignored.

I close with a story not yet mentioned. Historically, eye care was a turf war between the ophthalmologist and the optometrist. Years before most of these professionals dreamed of working together, our ophthalmologist-led department recognized the foolishness of this battle and acknowledged the great value of strong optometry care. To really live our mission and take care of patients across all our communities, both roles were required. We needed to coordinate the two professions, and the clinicians needed to focus on something bigger than themselves. We had many highly successful clinicians. Our two groups of practitioners did not lack for ability, ego, or strength. Together, they did what many said could not be done. They deeply integrated and coordinated their respective specialties to provide a broad spectrum of eye care across a wide geographic area, and they endured even through the wild swings in the economics of healthcare. They were both close to the work, willing to work in a structure, and willing to go against conventional practice. The result was an amazingly strong department with great service and a quality of care for our communities that is rarely seen across the country.

Following these principles will not guarantee success or breakthrough innovations. What it should be able to do is help you attract values-driven staff, inspire them to create and contribute, and overcome barriers that leave others in the mediocre middle.

CHAPTER 8 TAKEAWAYS

- ☐ Innovation is not just for small teams or Silicon Valley garages.
- ☐ An organization can improve innovation by investing in leadership training that gets them close to the work and provides great tools.
- ☐ The management system should support, not thwart, innovation.
- ☐ The keys to innovation are:
  - ◦ Get close enough to the work to feel the moral imperative.
  - ◦ Use structure to improve innovation.
  - ◦ Maintain a disciplined disregard for conventional wisdom.

PART IV

COMMUNITY

CHAPTER 9

LEAD BEYOND
YOUR WALLS

*The measure of true success is the health
and well-being of the community.*

It is three o'clock in the morning, it's dark, and you are scared of what is happening with your six-year-old daughter. In one day, she has gone from a quiet, pleasant girl to a speechless, blank-eyed, non-responsive shadow of her former self. You hold her hand, but there is no response, no motion. Her arms and legs are stiff. You seek medical help. You hear the words "schizophrenia" and "psychotic break," and your past encounters with people, movies, and bits of information you have heard or read flood your brain. You are scared and unsure of what to do. Regardless of your work, your faith, your education—this experience will shake you.

And then the medical staff says that the hospital cannot admit your daughter, that it has no beds available in the psychiatric unit. They ask you to put your daughter in your car and drive three hours to a place that should be able to help her. In the most unsettling, unexpected, and unprepared-for moment in your life, you are told, "Sorry, good luck. We can't help you." This is so hard on families, so hard to solve, but this is the kind of struggle that defines organizations.

All of us have been touched by behavioral health or psychiatric problems, whether through our friends, coworkers, or our own families. Around the world, and certainly in the United States, the number of providers and spaces for patients with behavioral health issues has steadily decreased.[32] Many states now have only a fraction of the beds they need to give optimal care. The number of patients who need care far exceeds the capacity of providers or facilities. This is true for not only for patients in crisis but also for those with short-term or long-term needs. Our region was no different.

Ours was one of two hospitals in town that offered inpatient psychiatric care. Our unit was in a very old building that neither could nor should be expanded. It was not well put together, and the other hospital was in similar condition. The two organizations chose different paths. As demand rose and payments were reduced, the other organization chose to downscale services, hoping that the need would decrease or that others would pick up the slack. Like most behavioral health centers, it was losing money, so they steadily decreased the number of beds available. And when they had trouble recruiting doctors and other caregivers for the service, they decreased their capacity even further.

---

32   Victoria Bekiempis, "This Lack of Psychiatric Care Is Madness," Newsweek, December 11, 2013, www.newsweek.com/2013/12/13/lack-psychiatric-care-madness-244896.html; "Mental Health in America - Access to Care Data," MHA, www.mentalhealthamerica.net/issues/mental-health-america-access-care-data.

The ultimate measure of a man is not where he stands in moments of comfort and convenience, but where he stands at times of challenge and controversy.

—MARTIN LUTHER KING JR.

Let's go back to the nonresponsive six-year-old girl. Imagine that you are the leader of a healthcare organization or of its behavioral health department. What is your responsibility to that child, her family, and your community?

According to our mission statement, our responsibility was enormous. But, as with many clear paths forward, there were complications. At the time, our organization had committed to build a new replacement hospital. It was going to be the largest-ever capital expenditure for healthcare on our side of the state. We were barely coming out of the recession and, hoping to save the community money in a down market, decided to build then. The organization was stretched. Going back to the board to request a behavioral health center was a big stretch, indeed. But those most stretched were those suffering from mental issues and their families. We had to decide who was going to carry which part of the burden. If you went to the front lines, the decision was easy. Getting close to this work and seeing the patients of all ages who were about to be driven two, three hours away in the midst of a psychiatric crisis was gripping. It was true, there just wasn't anything available nearby. But it was also true that this was incredibly hard on patients and disruptive for their families.

The plan was to do something more than wring our hands. We had already increased our outpatient and daylong therapy activities, and we had put behavioral health providers into the primary care clinics. We coordinated care with others in community services to decrease the burden of psychiatric illness, but the numbers were just too great. So, in the face of what was happening across the whole region, we looked at it carefully and decided to keep our promises. The next step was clear—not easy, but clear.

Despite the fact that it was hard to recruit providers, and despite the fact that we might lose money on it, we decided to expand our services. A number of friends who were CEOs at the time said to me, "You're not thinking right, this is an area that often loses money, has complex legal issues . . . you should not do this." We knew that if we opened our doors and extended services to all without regard for payment, the service was at risk to lose money. But our plan rejected that risk as a certainty; our plan was to figure out how to deliver great care and break even. We weren't looking to make money on it, just to break even.

As an alternative, others suggested an equally unacceptable solution. "Well, of course you could build a new facility but you certainly should build it away from your campus, like out on the edge of town. So when you decide to not be in that business at a future date, you can just cut it loose and it won't be a problem." We didn't believe that was a reasonable plan, either. We were in the business of taking care of people and our community. We felt we would always have patients with behavioral health problems. There was no reason we'd ever want to "cut it loose." We felt this initiative was an integral part of our mission to care for patients and the community. Our plan was to build it right on our campus. In fact, it was to be connected to all the other parts of our campus, just as behavioral health issues are connected to all the other issues that patients have. And we would neither separate it nor abandon it.

And here's where it connects to durability. We received pressure from outside advisors as noted. We also had pushback from a strong, thoughtful board member who said, "Yes, long term it makes sense, but we don't want to do it now. We are doing too many things, taking too many risks." Although many agreed with those concerns, the need to serve the community, give our staff better tools, and, most importantly, take some of the burden from families at a most difficult time convinced the majority to move ahead with the plan.

We will delve a bit deeper into this undertaking later, but one last important note: This decision was about the community, so we felt it would be important to let them in on what we planned, built, and implemented. Right before patients were to be admitted, we invited the community to come and see what the facility looked and felt like.

We have all held or visited open houses. However, this one was unique. We had two thousand people from the community walk through this new thirty-bed behavioral health hospital. We had staff members stand up and talk about what goes on there. In contrast to every other open house we have had, we received not a single comment or complaint from the public worrying about wasting money on facilities. Two thousand people from the community came and no one complained to me about our spending resources on behavioral health.

The mix of visitors was broad: neighbors, teachers, politicians, business leaders, and people from the faith community. A number of visitors pulled me aside and said, "Jeff, you don't know this, but my son/wife/brother/friend has had a serious problem and it's so great to see you guys are stepping up, even though I know it's not the most popular thing to do these days." I told them all that our board chose to not be in it for the money or popularity, but to serve the patients and their families.

It was a great success that held true to our principles and bucked conventional wisdom, which would be to stay out of the risky behavioral health business and let somebody else handle the problem—as if there was anyone else out there who would do this. We felt we were in the best position to fill this critical need, and we stepped up and did it. One of the clear markers that separates good organizations from great organizations is figuring out how to not only survive but to thrive. We had the discipline to expand and fill a need, and we believed that we could deliver better care for those in need without losing money. It was not an easy endeavor, but it was an opportunity to distinguish ourselves and show what living true to our values looked like.

The best way for an organization to motivate a community is to live a motivated life among them.

The only way to motivate people is to live a motivated life in front of them.

—BILL HYBELS

OUTSIDE THE WALLS, OUTSIDE THE RULES

Behavioral health issues aren't the only ones pressing on families, organizations, and communities. Many businesses and agencies have long noticed that a small percentage of the population uses a disproportionate amount of healthcare. Five percent of the population uses 50 percent of all the healthcare dollars in the United States. Some find themselves among that 5 percent due to one-time catastrophic events like a heart attack or a car accident, but many are the sickest, most complicated patients and have multiple, often recurring, problems. They see their primary care providers and multiple specialists, use many public services, and strain the healthcare budgets of their families or employers. One of the sad truths is that healthcare has not made improving the care of this population a priority because it has not been pressed financially to do so. Most healthcare still gets paid to take care of sick people, not to keep them healthy.

The question is, do you follow your values, or do you follow the money? To follow your values, you will have to spend money to keep people healthier, which means you get less revenue. To address this complex issue, we used the best data, and some of our best staff, to help guide these patients along their way. We felt we could markedly improve and maintain their health and prevent the need for many tests and trips to the hospital. It could decrease the communities' healthcare costs and improve the patients' experiences.

We implemented that model of focused care coordinators with great success in keeping patients healthier and helping them live fuller lives. We spent several million dollars each year for a system that decreased our revenue by tens of millions of dollars. Making organizational decisions consistent with our values makes it more likely that staff will make decisions consistent with our values. In chapter 5, we talked about building an environment with an expectation of service. The following is a great example of what living our values and delivering a great level of service to a member of the community feels like.

Ethel was a quiet but strong-willed ninety-four-year-old. She would not take her meds, neither would she eat what she needed to. She no longer even cared to play her father's violin, which had been one of her great joys. The diagnosis: her long-term, closest companion, a dog named Baby, had died. Ethel's nurse care coordinator, Deb Arentz, recognized just how important Ethel's dog had been to her. She wondered whether Ethel could manage a dog if she found one for her. Then she spotted an advertisement: the owner of a small-breed dog, a Shih Tzu, could no longer care for her and was looking for a good home. It seemed like a perfect match.

It was love at first sight for Ethel, who also named this dog Baby (Ethel's friends were amused because she wouldn't allow reference to Baby's breed because she thought "Shih Tzu" sounded like cursing).

"She loved that dog. The dog would sit with her on the back of her chair or sit next to her on the piano bench when she played," Deb said. "Being ninety-four-years-old, she had a lot of aches and pains, but the dog allowed her to focus on something else."

A few weeks later, a rejuvenated Ethel had gained weight and was able to walk 125 feet at a time, a big improvement from sitting all day. One morning she arrived at Gundersen with her violin, which she opened and played in the hospital lobby for patients, staff, and visitors.

"It just meant the world to us as caregivers," Deb said. "It was a little thing in the whole scope of her issues, but to Ethel and her family, it was a big thing. This dog was absolutely crucial for her quality of life."

It was a great outcome. This coordinator had helped to provide her with real joy when days before there was none. All this was made possible by a staff member acting on her own, but still acting in concert with the values of the organization to serve a higher purpose.

What's the financial return on that? There is none. But that story went around our organization and got highlighted as an example of truly listening to the patient and going outside our walls to serve. Later this story was told at an IHI national convention with five thousand people attending from all around the country. Thousands more from around the world would be hearing about the character of our staff—what it looks like and feels like to live the mission.

People knew that we were not getting paid for that effort. As for a return on investment, to have selfless service called out on local and national stages helps to solidify the culture and build momentum. How much is it worth to have a leader from Stanford meet one of our directors at that same conference and have him say, "Oh, you're from Gundersen? You guys are so great!" That director later recalled that encounter at a leadership meeting with two hundred colleagues. That kind of recognition is something you can't measure in dollars and cents.

Of course, our care coordinators do far more than deliver dogs. They make a significant difference in preventing illness and complications and managing costs. Our program spent more than $2 million a year on staff expenses that saved the community tens of millions of dollars by preventing illness, surgeries, and return hospitalizations that would have otherwise been needed. That doesn't seem like a very smart move for a health system. But our values demanded that we treat everyone the same, without regard for the payment classification or our profit margins.

Here's another example: Mike is a nice man with obesity, diabetes, and congestive heart failure. His care coordinators would check on him regularly to make sure he was weighing himself as planned. One day, he failed to report as scheduled, so they called him to see if he was okay. No response. They called again—no response. Worried, the care coordinator kept trying until she was finally able to reach him. She discovered that Mike had not called in because he was embarrassed. He had eaten three pieces of pie at a church potluck and was now eight pounds heavier! He wanted to wait until his weight went down to call.

But it wasn't the pie (although three pieces might be a bit more than any of us should have at a sitting). Mike was gaining weight because his heart failure was worsening. Without intervention, he would likely keep putting on water weight and end up in the emergency department or possibly the ICU. With intervention from the nurse and the advising clinician, his medications were changed, his weight was monitored every day, and he was put back on a path to his usual state of health, escaping the downward spiral. Investing in staff and structure to keep patients healthier shows true commitment to values-based leadership.

This model has evolved in many other organizations, but always with the theme of moving farther outside the walls of the hospitals and clinics, into the patients' lives. Not all have used nurses or social workers. There are great examples of using pre-med students, nursing students, and trained community health workers to similar ends.[33] All of these examples involve moving beyond what traditional healthcare has focused on in order to improve the community health as a whole.

Beyond behavioral health and complex care, obesity looms as a major strain on the health and well-being of our communities. This is another chance to decide whether you will lead, follow, or ignore an issue that wreaks havoc across all of society. The issue is complex and seemingly insurmountable—there is no easy fix. That alone could be used as an excuse to let someone else take it on or focus energy elsewhere. But if we were really going to attempt to improve the health and well-being of the communities, then we needed to act.

In the 1980s we started addressing the issue. One problem we noticed was that postoperative heart patients often return to many of the same problematic habits that put them in such bad shape to

---

33   Rachel Garza, "Prescription for a Healthier Community," Allegheny College, November 14, 2013, http://sites.allegheny.edu/news/2013/11/14/pre-scription-for-a-healthier-community/; "A Community Health Worker Training Resource," CDC, October 6, 2016, www.cdc.gov/dhdsp/programs/spha/chw_training/.

begin with. We teamed our leading nutrition expert with our clinical staff to develop a food scorecard, examining what was in specific foods and then suggesting portion sizes for those foods. This evolved into a program called the 500 Club. It centered on meals with 500 calories in a balanced nutritional profile. This doesn't sound so revolutionary now, but it was developed because this information was just not available at the time. Many institutions started working on this for their patients, but to really make an impact, we took the program outside the walls of the hospital to traditional and fast food restaurants, convenience stores, and even a baseball park.

As a true compliment, it was copied and spread across hundreds of venues. The 500 Club was not guaranteed to fix the problem— you could always eat three of the 500-calorie offerings at the same time—but it started thousands of conversations across all parts of food delivery on improving approaches to food service and eating. We could not have done this by ourselves. We had many strong partners to set an example and to support the program, despite the risk to their business. Dave Skogen (grocery stores, chapter 8) and Don Weber (LHI, chapter 4), true to form and consistent with their values, were happy to participate.

These efforts were important but only part of the package. As the obesity rate in children exploded, our executive chef left the kitchen and set up classes in many of the local schools to teach the joys of cooking and eating healthy, locally grown foods. It has been a big success and has inspired parents to rethink what they are buying and eating. To stay consistent with what we were teaching our children, the health system had to change, as well. With a moderate amount of angst, we changed what we served to our staff and patients. We wanted to buy more local food to help the regional economy, but we found that community agriculture models don't work so well for large organizations. Instead, we became partners and initial investors with a co-op organized by Sue Noble called the Fifth Season. The co-op buys locally and provides a source from which hospitals and large schools can purchase regional products.

But it takes more than knowledge and making better food available to tackle obesity. We, like many others, had programs for weight management. We listened to the participants, and in response to their requests, we sponsored classes for men, women, and children, as well as pre- and post-partum women. We aimed to decrease the barriers and increase the participation. We measured and published outcomes, we changed and modified our approach, but we always tried to tie it together as a total package.[34] Did any of these efforts make money for us? No. But, they were an integral part of our overall plan to improve the population's health.

When these programs were insufficient for some patients, we also had a surgical option for obesity. Yes, we could make a profit on some of those patients, but our approach was to embed this option as part of our overall community plan—ranging from the least intrusive solutions to more intervention, as needed. When we established the surgical program, it was done in a disciplined, thoughtful, and well-monitored fashion. Thoughtful scientific criteria, not just a checkbook, got you in line for surgery. With the program's focus on outcomes and well-being of the patients, its long-term results are the best of any program willing to submit to peer review.[35]

---

34   Schauberger C.W., Rooney B.L., Brimer L.M., "Factors that influence weight loss in the puerperium," *Obstetrics & Gynecology* no. 49, 3: 424–429; B.L. Rooney and C.W. Schauberger, "Excess pregnancy weight gain and long-term obesity: One decade later," *Obstetrics & Gynecology* no. 100, 2 (2002): 245–252.

35   Shanu N. Kothari, Andrew J. Borgert, Kara J. Kallies, Matthew T. Baker, Brandon T. Grover, "Long-term (>10-year) outcomes after laparoscopic Roux-en-Y gastric bypass," *Surgery for Obesity and Related Diseases,* December 22, 2016, http://dx.doi.org/10.1016/j.soard.2016.12.011.

A comprehensive look outside the normal boundaries compelled us to partner with others to take on pressing, life-altering issues. The requirement for courage was not so big, but there was an important need to be disciplined, to follow through, measure, and ensure that we were accomplishing something, not just doing something.

The final area to mention is the responsibility to our neighborhood. Where you live or play is always important. Our organizations live in neighborhoods and provide another opportunity to live our values. Will trees and bushes add dollars to your bottom line? Probably not much, but they can change the attitude of your staff, the customers or patients who interact with your staff, and those that pass by or live in your neighborhood. Small things done well can have a big impact.

We were given a large warehouse next to campus. At one time, it had been a nice-looking, three-story building, but now it was ragged and worn, plagued with asbestos, and an electrical and plumbing nightmare. To tear it down would have been expensive, but to even make it into a workable storage facility was going to cost several million dollars. We studied what other communities had done. In the process, we found a group that would seek out a variety of funding streams to refurbish and expand old buildings that were potentially historically significant. It sounded great. The one catch was that the investment stream required that a significant portion of the building be used as subsidized housing for low-income tenants.

On the surface, that was not a problem. The neighborhood was in need of housing for people of modest income. Many of our employees could qualify, and it all seemed consistent with our mission to improve our community. But many on the board were worried. The renovation seemed like a great idea, but the low-income housing was a big red flag to them. What if it worked out poorly? What if the building was not kept up well? What if the tenants became a problem for our staff? None of the board members lived in the neighborhood. They really wanted to do what was best for the organization and the community, but they were worried about the risk.

At this juncture, a long discussion about our mission and values was not nearly as valuable as a road trip. Jerry Arndt, who you met in chapter 5, was now our SVP of business. He was all-in on this project and came up with the idea to rent a bus and bring the board to go and see for themselves. After an all-day, nearly five-hundred-mile adventure, they came back complaining that we were not moving along fast enough and asking whether there was an opportunity to make the building bigger. What they had seen were well-maintained former schools and factories that were now thriving as mixed-income housing.

We moved ahead and allowed a portion of our campus to be used for the well-being of our neighborhood. Years later, as you might expect, the property is filled with people of all incomes and backgrounds, is well maintained, and has helped inspire further development. Also in the neighborhood, one developer is building modest but nice medical resident housing and another group is building a hotel, which is to be followed by a restaurant, grocery store, and additional housing. Our contributions to these endeavors have not been out of our patients' pockets. We have found local and regional partners to provide the needed capital. On one edge of our campus, an empty, storm-damaged, former-factory is being turned into apartments. On the other edge of campus, two parks have been refurbished. Finally, we have formed a joint development corporation with the city, each contributing and sharing equal say in how best to spend funds to improve the neighborhood.

Because of the strength of our organization and our steadfast commitment to our values, outside partners are willing to make long-term investments. Together we have honored the promise of our mission to the community.

CHAPTER 9 TAKEAWAYS

☐ Great organizations live their values despite inconvenience or cost—they find a way.

☐ Staff will follow an organization's lead to live their values.

☐ Tackling obesity was a problem bigger than any single organization or program, requiring partnerships across the community, diversity of approach, and the discipline to follow through.

☐ Our values would require we act when there is a need, not just when it is convenient.

☐ Find the joy and value in improving the health and well-being of one person at a time, even if the whole system is in need of change.

☐ Use your assets of consistency and a commitment to a higher cause to bring like-minded partners to the table.

☐ The best way for an organization to motivate a community is to live a motivated life among them.

CHAPTER 10

FUNDS AND FOUNDATIONS TO SERVE YOUR VALUES

Finances and facilities are tools— important, useful tools, but just tools.

Here is your chance. You can do great good for the community, change the lives of many, distinguish your organization, and set the tone for the future. All you have to do is risk your career, find tens of millions of dollars you don't think you have, and convince a group of very thoughtful, well-meaning board members who think you may have lost your senses.

We first met Don Weber, CEO of Logistics Health, Inc. (LHI), in chapter 2. He and his partners had taken a local start-up from a couple million dollars in revenue per year to a $100 million high-tech service organization. They developed a system that saved the military money and greatly improved the percentage of men and women who were ready to be deployed. LHI had grown rapidly and had added hundreds of high-paying jobs into the community. La Crosse's population is just over fifty thousand, so hundreds of high-paying tech jobs with outside money coming into the community was a huge boon. Furthermore, Don and his wife, Roxie, had emerged as one of the most significant philanthropic families in the community—not because they were the richest but because they were extremely generous and had a sharp focus on trying to improve the community.

So, where is the potentially career-ending problem? As you might recall, LHI's president and CEO had come to Gundersen and asked that we invest tens of millions of dollars to keep LHI in La Crosse. It was an extraordinary request. Most would have turned it down flat out and many in our organization suggested we do just that. As you know from chapter 2, the stakes were extraordinarily high for the community, for Gundersen, and for our leadership. Failure would taint much of the organization's progress and solidify the narrow thinking and preconceived ideas of what the boundaries of our caring activity should be. But we believed that our financial risk was manageable and that our investment would not only help the community but would also inspire other investors to put money into the community.

Where did we get the money? Like most organizations, we have gold in our basement. Not gold bars, of course, but assets stranded by rigid thinking about how capital should be invested. Most have it in the usual stocks and bonds, treasury notes, and some cash. Owing to our mission, ours was spread over a pretty secure distribution. With the purchase of a large portion of LHI, we had committed to invest some of our savings locally rather than securely in the usual—but minimally beneficial—portfolio.

The community was surprised and mostly pleased by our decision. Many business people and community members hailed it as a breakthrough, recognizing a commitment to the community unlike they'd ever seen. We were a big organization using its power and savings to build the community, as opposed to just keeping our money stored "in the basement." We took the risk to act on our values to serve the greater good.

Sixteen months after we made this monumental investment, we found a well-suited buyer who would keep LHI in our community. The return was stunning on all fronts. Our financial return was more than five times what our stock and bonds portfolio made over that same sixteen months. LHI was able to stay and grew as promised. To this day, the Webers and their staff continue to be an integral part of the health, well-being, and growth in the region.

The money for this initiative did not come from an outside source; it came from thinking differently. It came from understanding that 100 percent of our assets don't need to be stuck in large, distant funds. Indeed, a portion can be used in disciplined, thoughtful, and well-vetted investments in regional opportunities that are consistent with our purpose and values.

Another example of using our assets to serve the community can be found in our goals for mitigating our impact on the environment. This endeavor included lowering the cost of care, improving the local economy, as well as decreasing our illness-causing pollution. With millions of square feet, seven thousand employees, and endless technology to heat, cool, and power, we had a big challenge that would take a significant investment. Would we make patients pay more? Would we make employers pay more? Both were bad options.

Although smaller investments, such as waste reduction efforts, were taken out of operations funds (with a 60 percent yearly financial return on investment), large investments came from savings. We chose to invest in local infrastructure rather than tying up all our funds in stocks and bonds. In all, only about 5 percent of our savings was invested in this fashion, but it yielded internationally famous results. This is not giving away assets needed to secure bond documents or meet financial requirements; this is using a portion of savings for the direct good of the community.

Is Gundersen the only organization with assets that could be put to use? Certainly not. Ours is a tiny nugget in a very large basement of gold. In 2015, the Federal Reserve said that non-financial institutions were holding more than $3.5 trillion in cash. At the same time, hedge funds and private equity cash holdings were another $10 trillion. Even a tiny portion of these funds would be a huge boost to communities these institutions operate in. An outstanding description and detail of these concepts can be found in *The New Grand Strategy*.[36] The authors describe in great detail these "stranded assets" and the opportunity they offer.

"Success comes to those who have an entire mountain of gold that they continually mine, not those who find one nugget and try to live on it for fifty years."

—JOHN C. MAXWELL

---

36   Mark Mykleby, Patrick Doherty, and Joel Makower, *The New Grand Strategy* (St. Martin's Press, 2016).

WASTE: THE GREAT OPPORTUNITY

That's a good start, but there's much more gold available if we are willing to dig for it. In most organizations, *waste* is a stranded asset of equal size but much different shape. In healthcare, the estimates are 20 to 50 percent waste.[37] I did a very unscientific study to document this fact several years ago. I was sitting at a table with four young physicians in training who had no time to read books like this and asked them if they thought there was 20 percent waste in healthcare. They fell off their chairs laughing. They said it wasn't anywhere near 20 percent; in truth, they said, it was closer to 50 percent. Even if it were only half of that, 25 percent, there was a great opportunity to free up more capital. The percentage of waste will vary by organization, but the opportunity to save money will be great.

In addition, there is growing evidence in business and government that attacking waste can improve your staff's morale, as well as your department or organization's finances.[38] Maureen Bisognano is a master at helping others spot the always-present waste. This takes us back to our discussion in chapter 5 about tools. The CAP from GE can be used to develop a shared need by all staff. We used tools like the A3 to let them describe their current reality and build better possibilities. We engaged with IHI to continuously measure, improve, and build on previous changes. We believed that one of the biggest wastes is not using the talents of your staff—not asking or listening to their insights, or asking them to correct errors that the system could have been set up to avoid in the first place. These tools were invaluable in facilitating this. Failure to take your staff and

---

37   "Health Policy Brief," Health Affairs, December 13, 2012, http://healthaffairs.org/healthpolicybriefs/brief_pdfs/healthpolicybrief_82.pdf.

38   Maureen Bisognano and Charles Kenney, *Pursuing the Triple Aim* (Jossey-Bass, 2012).

their talents into account is indeed a form of waste: a waste of time, energy, and enthusiasm.

SET THE TONE—DRIVE TO THE OUTCOME

One more concept to consider when finding a way forward with your own organization is committing to a firm goal in a firm timeline. To merely make money turns out to be a short-lived and hollow goal for many. But using those funds for a higher purpose can move the crowd. How difficult the goal is not the key; it's how hard you persist that determines success. For example, to help keep public costs down, we set a goal to keep our annual fee increases less than the year before. The fee was still rising but in ever-smaller increments. This goal sent a clear message to the public but also to the staff: We were not going to solve our financial problems on the backs of our patients. We were going to find other ways—internal ways—to address our problems. Waste reduction was vital to this idea. This was a clear, relentless, and determined goal, unique among our peers. It was also a source of difficulty but ultimately became a source of pride for the staff.

FISCAL DISCIPLINE

A Success Story: Declining Fee Increase Trend

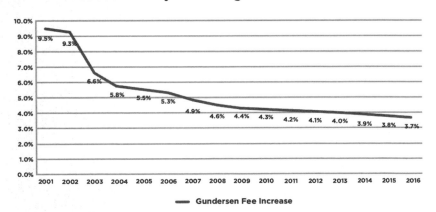

The message was clear that we were working to improve the well-being of the community. We showed a determination to live our values and, at the same time, move to higher performance and better fiscal sufficiency. We set this steady downward path for fee increases (below the state average for fourteen years), despite getting paid by Medicare in the lowest first percentile in the country and having one of the lowest Medicaid reimbursement rates in the country.[39] Did our infrastructure suffer? No. We were able to obtain newer buildings, newer IT, and three times the savings we had prior to beginning our efforts. We had the courage to set the goal, the discipline to make it work, and the durability to stay with it through tough times. Had we set less-inspiring goals, we would have been unlikely to realize those outcomes.

However, finances are not the mission—they help us serve the mission. Likewise, facilities are not the endpoints—they are tools that help us reach our goals.

FACILITIES ARE TOOLS

For years, our medium-sized, tertiary hospital at Gundersen had garnered awards for excellent outcomes. Those awards were for the amazing work people had done inside those walls, despite how antiquated those hospital walls were. Unfortunately, the hospital was falling apart. For years, CEOs and senior leaders had patched and fixed, added a bit here, and improved the surface there, but the facility in which our staff was taking care of patients was in worse shape than many of the community hospitals in the nineteen-county region from which those patients had been transferred. The aging

---

39   "Dartmouth Atlas of Health Care," 2017, www.dartmouthatlas.org.

facility required many workarounds and much extra effort by the staff, and it offered little space for families.

Why had the building not been replaced? The organization had done well. It could have borrowed the money, and it could have gotten help from the community. Among the largest of the many distracting priorities was fear—fear of failing in public. Many of us will put off big projects, even badly needed projects, to avoid the attendant risk. With an uncertain economy and a hard-to-predict future, taking on a massive, capital-intensive project could end badly. Potential hazards include unanticipated delays, cost overruns, and interdepartmental competition for the new space—more risk and headaches than many are willing to take on.

Another impediment was the prevailing wisdom by most experts in healthcare policy at the time. With changes in clinical practice, the number of inpatient beds needed across the country was far less than the number of beds in service. Much was being written about the shift from inpatient to outpatient care and the inevitable decreased need for hospital beds. Were we really going to add beds to a bed glut? Conventional wisdom was that this was not a wise financial move.

We spent a great deal of time planning a great place for patients and families, as well as our staff—whether that meant renovation or a new build. With the help of General Electric, we studied our workflows. We projected near- and far-term types and volumes of patients. Ultimately, we decided to build a replacement hospital—not to dominate the world, or to increase our market share, but to use as a tool to improve the health and well-being of our community and our staff.

We decided to build because patients, families, and the entire region needed a better facility than even a complete renovation of the old facility could provide. Patients and staff were consulted at every point along the way to ensure that the new building would be an efficient space and, most importantly, a healing place. The new hospital has many open-air spaces, large windows, plenty of room for families to stay, lifts for patients with disabilities, and an easy-access design that allows nurses to do their work while disturbing patients and their families as little as possible. Building a new hospital had nothing to do with broad healthcare policies or politics; it was all about how to take care of patients who were begging to come to our facility for their care.

Around the country, the number of patients needing hospitalization was declining. Despite that, our numbers steadily rose. Sick patients were coming from miles and miles away saying, "This is where I want to be cared for because I feel really cared for here. And my family feels cared for." The new facility was serving as a tool to deliver that care. When I spoke with patients and families, they would tell me that the hospital was very nice, but almost always they would add that the people were great. If you give staff tools and a values-based structure in which to function, they can deliver amazing care.

What about the financial risk? This new facility came in exactly on time and tens of millions of dollars under budget, partially because we had the courage to build it in the midst of a recession. To be clear, borrowing was less expensive during the economic downturn, and we saved some on copper, steel, glass, and other commodities. But where we really saved money was on people—and I do not mean on their salaries.

The workers who were available to work on this facility were drawn from the best construction teams all over our region. Many highly skilled tradespeople were sitting on the sidelines, unemployed because of the downturn in construction. So when contractors went looking for welders or electricians to take on this giant project, they found the best.

We had amazing people on our construction team. They helped solve or avoid problems, and they helped us save tens of millions of dollars. Did we have good architects and senior staff? Sure, our director of construction and project management, Kari Houser, and her team were disciplined, smart, durable, and important to our success. But our frontline construction people, most of whom were from our own region, were also outstanding in how hard they worked, how smart they were, and how many problems they solved.

Great vision without great people is irrelevant.
—JAMES COLLINS

The people of our region built a fabulous facility in which they and their families could receive care for decades to come. And they did it exactly as it needed to be done, serving the patients and the staff and finishing on time and remarkably under budget. It's a good thing, because building new facilities is expensive for communities, and operating them over the next three to five decades will be even more expensive. We paid for this effort with savings, borrowings, and philanthropy. Despite the tough economy, the campaign to build our replacement hospital attracted more donors and more million-dollar-plus donations than any other effort of any kind in our region. Why? For love of bricks and steel and glass? No, for the programs, the people, and the sense that we were truly living up to our commitment of serving the well-being of the community.

MORE PARTNERS, MORE FUNDING

Through the funding of various initiatives, we welcomed many partners, but one notable partnership was with our city government. Many cities are now very short on funds, yet face the need to revitalize poorer sections of their communities. To entice people to build in struggling neighborhoods, cities often use a common tool called tax increment financing, or *TIF*. Under TIF, taxes are forgiven for a time to get a project up and running, and eventually the city benefits from the improved tax base and additional jobs. The City of La Crosse was strapped for funds, so rather than postpone taxes under the TIF, we agreed to pay in the property taxes immediately, with the understanding that the city would eventually return the money to us as reward for building our new facilities in a distressed neighborhood rather than in the more affluent suburbs. It was a good plan. But the payments didn't come, and the agreement terms were in turmoil.

A potential court battle loomed, a scenario that neither we nor the city wanted. Instead, we allowed La Crosse to delay payment, and we decreased our share by 15 percent. That 15 percent would go into a pool of funds matched by the city for large neighborhood improvements—parks and walkways, property to erect new affordable housing, and seed money to attract other willing investors. Our dollar investment was minimal, but this agreement was one of the reasons we were able to entice others to consider building that long list of neighborhood improvements noted in chapter 9 (hotel, restaurant, grocery store, apartments). This cooperation and commitment to the long term was a clear signal that we and the city were working well together, had formed and started to implement a long-term plan, and were complementing each other to serve the good of the public.

MORE PARTNERS, BETTER USE OF FUNDS

Urban health disparities and outcomes are issues of immense impact on urban populations. Less talked about, but of equal concern, is the health and well-being across rural areas.

Blanche was an elderly woman living with her elderly sister in a tiny, rural, American town. Although she was isolated from big-city strife, she also was one of the millions isolated from access to basic health screening and treatments. Not only is local healthcare in these rural areas insufficient or nonexistent, but limited transportation options also restrict access to more distant care. If care is available, it is usually not affiliated with multispecialty healthcare centers or testing facilities. Children particularly fare poorly in rural areas. But Blanche and those in her age group fare even worse: Compared with their urban counterparts, they are poorer, older, and less insured but have more issues with alcohol, tobacco, and obesity.[40]

The question placed on the table for many health and civic organizations is what to do about an obvious issue affecting tens of millions? If you are a leader whose values include compassion and integrity, then it is difficult to look the other way. There are diseases that could be prevented, suffering that could be decreased, and lives that could be enriched if we could find the courage to tackle these disparities. Many looking at the same picture have defaulted to the let-somebody-else-do-it stance, while others believe that having rural populations come to the city would be more effective and efficient.

The question then becomes, more efficient for whom? More importantly, more effective for whom? We have found that the less convenient, the greater the distance, and the more complicated the system, the more people—especially the elderly—will not be

---

40   "Dartmouth Atlas of Health Care," 2017, www.dartmouthatlas.org.

screened, will not follow up, and will not get the care they need to stay healthy or to manage their chronic health problems.

Whether you act on this great need will be determined by whether you have the courage to act on your values, the discipline to develop a system that works, and the durability to survive the internal struggles and external criticism.

By now you will not be surprised that Gundersen took on this problem with a long-term community-building approach. It began with innovation by connecting information on the clinic side. For instance, a paper medical record in a hospital is cumbersome, clumsy, and inefficient. But in the outpatient rural areas, a paper record is a disaster. It leaves no understanding of what happened at another clinic or at any one of several hospitals at which a patient may have been seen over the years. And even if the primary care doctor has some basic information from the specialists, the specialists almost never have information from each other.

Chaos and confusion—what a perfect place to start! This was an area where we could do the most good for those in the most need.

We built our own medical record to serve all of our clinics and specialty clinics and to have available in the tertiary hospital. We added laboratory and radiology results to minimize duplication of testing and to make it easier for everyone to know what tests others had performed and what the results were. Not long thereafter, we added telemedicine to connect across a wide geography and make care more efficient for all. Was this innovation going to make tons of money? Not likely. But innovation to deliver care closer to our standard of excellence—that would keep costs down and keep people healthier—served the greater good of our communities. Our plan was not to support the status quo; rather, it was to have an innovative but disciplined approach to change.

But what about the community hospital? Blanche remembers when babies were delivered and surgeries performed there; the lives of one relative or another had been saved, or at least greatly aided, by that local hospital. But times change. Recruiting providers into rural areas is tough, the cost of delivering excellent care is high, and the finances are heavily stacked against success. Once again, it's easy to say, "Just have people go to the big tertiary center." It's much harder to ask, what is the *best* model, not the easiest model, but the best model to serve our communities? We gathered local clinical staff, community members, healthcare delivery experts, and infrastructure support leaders to build a plan that would deliver the best outcome for the most people.

The undertaking was rigorous. First we threw out the conventional wisdom that competition will solve all quality and cost problems in all settings. We believed that in healthcare some regions are so small that competition will push resources to a point of diminishing returns and it will not be sustainable for either organizations or communities. We combined clinics, hospitals, laboratories, radiology, and inpatient and outpatient services into one organization.

Competition makes things come out, right? Well, what does that mean in healthcare? More hospitals so they compete with each other; more doctors compete with each other. More pharmaceutical companies. We set up a war. Wait a minute, let's talk about the patient. The patient doesn't need a war!

—DON BERWICK

To truly serve the public and expand access to care, we decided we should do only those things we can do very well. We had to decide what services should be cut and what should be enhanced. We did not want to do things just because they were easy money-makers or because something was being well reimbursed by payment systems. And we certainly didn't want to do things that were based largely on emotional or historical connections. Things like babies: everyone likes to have babies being born in their facilities, but if you cannot adequately cover for emergencies, if you cannot prove that your outcomes are as good as or better than if mothers and babies were going elsewhere, then you shouldn't be delivering babies. Delivering babies and a variety of other services that met the we-can't-do-it-well-enough criterion had to be discontinued. That was not easy, and it was not pleasant. It took discipline to stick with our promise and focus only on what we were going to do well. We wanted to prove our outcomes, not just advertise them. We wanted to be known for those things we did well.

The results have been fantastic: better quality, better service, and better access to preventive screening and specialists. And these results are now being replicated at multiple sites. As for the economist who still believes that competition is the only way to serve the public, there is another way: disciplined, values-driven healthcare that commits to the measurable well-being of the community—the whole community, including its financial health. For Gundersen and these regional sites, quality is up, service is up, efficiency and trust are up, and fee increases are down; the public is well served. We had the courage to take this on and the durability to make it work well for all.

Small-market competition is best replaced by disciplined, values-driven systems that commit to transparent, measurable improvements in the community's well-being.

There are many opportunities to work with like-minded, values-driven teams in and beyond your community. If they share your values but come from a different sector of society, all the better. Collaboration will multiply your investment faster than the stock market.

THINK DIFFERENTLY

Keeping LHI in the region was a noble goal. Many would have shaken their head, wrung their hands, and wished for a solution before shrugging it off. But our board chose to find a way. Think differently. Align your priorities differently. Decide how you can help the most people for the longest time and then find the courage to act. Decreasing waste takes less courage but also requires much discipline and a great deal of durability. Decreasing waste means changing how we do our work. Sometimes we need to force the issue with a goal aimed at something bigger than ourselves, such as lower fees for the community. We found assets in a willing—not wealthy but willing—governmental partner with the same desires but a markedly different structure with whom we shared common ground and values.

There are many sources of funds and many uses of facilities. The theme is to use your values and your creativity to look for solutions outside mainstream thinking. Conventional wisdom is often not wisdom at all. Partnering with a financially strapped city leadership with the same priorities resulted in great progress. We built the behavioral health hospital going against the common trend, our electronic health records started in the rural and outpatient clinics in opposition to the common trend, and we supported—not abandoned—redesigned regional centers and built a new hospital in the face of an economic downturn. These are all examples of using finances and facilities as tools to meet our goals. They served as critical tools to accomplish our mission and live our values. But in the end, they were really just tools to serve the greater good.

In the next chapter, we will put our values, principles, and assets on the line once again to show how we can serve the health of the community, improve our region's environment, lower costs of doing business, and improve the local economy, all at the same time.

CHAPTER 10 TAKEAWAYS

- ☐ Explore multiple paths to find the resources you need.
- ☐ Investment in the community can pay large dividends, often financial.
- ☐ Long-term, disciplined investment beyond the usual avenues is a great strategy for organizations and communities.
- ☐ Find your gold, use your assets. Partners with the same values are one of those available assets.
- ☐ Facilities and finances are tools—important tools, but tools.
- ☐ Innovation and discipline can work past conventional wisdom to serve the mission.
- ☐ A commitment to your values means remaining committed all the time, not just when it is convenient.

CHAPTER 11

LEAD THE MORAL AND FINANCIAL CASE FOR A BETTER ENVIRONMENT

Decrease costs, improve the economy, and protect our health.

What if you could have a significant impact on people's lives and your community by advocating for environmentally sensible reforms in your industry? What if such an undertaking came with considerable professional risk and a significant likelihood of failure? What if taking the right course meant losing money and possibly alienating companies you needed to work with? Would you have the courage and durability to live true to your values and pursue monumental change regardless of the consequence?

Gary Cohen is the founder and president of Healthcare Without Harm. For twenty years, this nongovernmental, not-for-profit organization has worked across the globe to decrease the enormous negative footprint of the healthcare industry on the environment.[41] For his ideas and his accomplishments, he is a MacArthur Genius Award recipient. He was a champion in the face of enormous adversity—a situation in which he could expect little help and massive resistance. What follows is the story about Gary's struggle to get the best products to take care of both patients and the environment.

About eight years ago, Gary's organization started a membership division called Practice Greenhealth, where hospitals and the companies that sold them products would have opportunities to learn from each other as they traveled together on the sustainability path.

"We were cautious about including these companies as members," Gary says, "because we knew from experience that they were principally interested in promoting and defending their products. We were especially concerned about including fossil fuel or chemical companies because, at their core, they are committed to continuing the petrochemical economy, which is in direct opposition to our mission."

The group's hospital members and its board, however, believed that there were progressive and innovative people in chemical companies who were trying to make the transition to green chemistry and align with the interests of the healthcare sector by detoxing their supply chain.

"Our members argued that we needed the chemical companies to make safer chemicals for them," Gary says, "and therefore they should

---

41   Health Care Without Harm, https://noharm.org/.

be allowed 'in the tent' as members and collaborators. Reluctantly, we agreed to include them as members in Practice Greenhealth."

Over the next few years, however, Gary began to doubt the wisdom of this decision. "We observed a few important signs," he says. "First, the chemical companies began to create doubt about our organizational decisions to highlight certain classes of chemicals for broad healthcare sector phase-out. This created confusion in our business membership in their efforts to demand safer chemicals in their products. Second, we observed that some companies were joining Practice Greenhealth to gain a 'green halo' and political cover—but they weren't really committed to sustainability in their product lines. This was not what we intended when we invited supply chain companies in as members!"

Gary was faced with a fork in the road. By this time, Practice Greenhealth had about ninety business members, and the dues they paid provided a significant income stream.

"I knew," Gary says, "that if we ended the business membership program, we would not only alienate many of these companies but also lose a lot of income."

Despite these very real and practical concerns, it was clear to Gary that the presence of certain companies in his organization was weakening Practice Greenhealth's focus and undermining the infrastructure of discipline that had made it a strong organization.

"I was deeply concerned," he says, "that continuing to include them would erode staff morale and lead to loss of credibility and effectiveness of our overall organization."

As the leader, Gary knew this was one of those times when, if his values mattered, he had to take action. Eventually, with the support of his board of directors, Gary was able to terminate the memberships of the supply-chain companies.

"Once we had made this decision," he says, "we embarked on a plan to develop a green purchasing cooperative in the health sector."

This for-benefit company, called Greenhealth Exchange, is designed to aggregate the collective purchasing power of hospital systems. It contracts for environmentally superior products and technologies for their hospital partners. In this way, Gary's organization could reward *products* rather than provide a green halo to entire companies.

Gary adds, "We could also create competition in the marketplace that would support a race to the top in service of healthier communities and a healthier planet."

Practice Greenhealth chose to suffer a major loss of income by eliminating an ethical conflict from its membership. Today, its plan is to grow the Greenhealth Exchange to help better find and develop products that are built safer, distributed with less impact, and easier to reuse or recycle.

Buying products already designed to recycle will give an added boost to the slowly growing recycling efforts across healthcare. Many organizations still have not gotten serious and are recycling only 10 to 15 percent of their purchased products. Through great effort, Gundersen's recycle-rate is above 40 percent, and we plan to increase that number to 80 percent. As an added bonus, we make a good profit on recycling and reusing. If set-in-their-ways doctors and nurses can make this work, I think anyone can.

GOING BEYOND TRADITIONAL PRACTICES

Remember our asthma patient in the chapter 8—the young boy who was once again in the ICU, struggling to breathe? The big question staring all of us in the face is what is our responsibility to that little boy and to all of those around us trying to breathe—to the millions who die of air quality issues each year? Do your values or those of your organization include the health of others? What if you are contributing to making them sick? Most of the heating, cooling, cooking, and transportation in the world involves burning fuels that foul the air and make it hard for people who have difficulty breathing.

As a healthcare organization, we knew our values were clear. How could we possibly continue harming the patients who we were trying so hard to help? Was it our responsibility to work for a cleaner environment? Without a doubt, yes.

In 2008, we learned that every year we were putting 434,000 pounds of particulate matter into the air by way of the coal burned for electricity and natural gas used for heating. At the same time, we put more than seventy-one million pounds of CO_2 into the atmosphere. Additionally, the coal that was burned deposited two pounds of mercury into our air, water, and land. Mercury —we all thought that we had gotten rid of that dangerous neurotoxin two decades ago, but here it was, and we were still causing it to spread.

Most people don't consider the impact healthcare has on the environment. Healthcare is more than twice as energy intensive as schools or offices. When you add in the impact of our complex technology and the massive pharmaceutical industry, we are a big problem. This raises a fundamental question we have asked several times: Is our role to focus 100 percent of our attention inside our walls, or do our values include the broader communities we serve?

We chose the latter. But to honor those values, we knew we had to take care of the whole of the community. We sought to not only decrease our impact on the environment but to do it in a way that would decrease costs to our patients and employers while improving the local economy. Improving the health and well-being of the community meant that we would take steps to help people breathe better and afford to breathe better. Notice the strategy: We did not allow ourselves to be bogged down by the global climate change controversy (even though the evidence of human effect on climate change is better than the evidence used to support many medical treatments). Instead, we chose to lead with local issues and local solutions. We did not wait for the federal government to solve this problem. We were certain that the problem and the solution could be framed by local data and local action.

Once again, going outside of traditional practices is cause for concern by staff and board members in many organizations. The key is to first find what priorities fit best with the organization's mission and values and to then have the courage to make the change.

Once we set down the path of lessening our environmental impact, we set a bold goal: be completely powered by renewable energy within eight years. We would not go into the high-priced "renewables" market to achieve our goal; instead, we would figure out a way (unknown to us at the time) to hit our energy mark, save Gundersen money, and improve the local economy. It was an outlandish goal but one that was community serving, not self serving. It was a risk to the organization and its leaders, but it was also a chance to help our community and teach others what is possible.

This was a huge plan for any board to get behind, so we softened the transition by focusing on early wins that we hoped would convince everyone that we could hit our goals. Decreasing our use of energy was the first and best choice. Changing light fixtures, pumps, and controls on heating and ventilating systems sounds like dull engineering work. It's certainly not sexy like wind turbines, and neither is it good for photo ops like sheets of solar panels, but it was great for decreasing costs and pollution.

This low-profile activity produced high-profile results. We spent $2 million dollars over eighteen months on those changes, and we have saved $1.2 million on energy costs every year since—a stunning return. Results were not only a 60 percent per year return on our investment but also much less pollution.[42]

Putting your money to work is better than leaving it in your savings accounts or in mutual funds, and it is better than letting it sit unused in your organization's basement. Even more money can be found by cutting waste. Over six years, our facilities decreased their energy consumption by 53 percent! That kind of decrease applied across healthcare and other sectors of the economy would create industry-changing savings. Healthcare alone spends $8 billion annually on energy. A 50 percent decrease could pay for tens of thousands of community nurses or help slow the rising cost of care.[43]

Not all of our efforts to improve sustainability turned out this well. Some, such as our wind turbines, which depended on the rate the power company paid us, struggled to break even. But even this modest success gave the board and our staff confidence that we could both save money and preserve the environment.

If we promised it, we planned to do it. We were not always completely sure how we were going to do it, but as Robert Service said, "A promise made is a debt unpaid."[44] To say we were going to measurably improve the local economy, we needed to do more than just keep the energy costs down on our hospitals and clinics. We chose to heat our major campus (4,500 staff, two hospitals, and many clinics)

---

42   Envision: Gundersen Health System, https://www.gundersenenvision.org/gundersen-envision/.

43   Direct Energy Business, "U.S. Healthcare Facilities Spend $8 Billion on Energy Each Year. Here's How They Can Save," April 8, 2016, https://business.directenergy.com/blog/2016/april/healthcare-energy-management.

44   Robert W. Service, "Cremation of Sam McGee."

with local wood chips from hardwood sawmills instead of natural gas. The overall cost of heating declined by hundreds of thousands of dollars, and what money we did spend went to local suppliers. The community quickly made the connection that burning fossil fuels from outside our area was expensive and unhealthy for our region. Replacing that energy supply with local renewables gave a nice boost to the local economy. Promise made and kept.

Solving multiple problems was a common theme. In a nearby county, phosphorus from dairy cow waste was hurting the lakes, and grease from restaurants was burdening the landfills. We took the manure from three dairies, along with tens of thousands of pounds of grease and other biowaste from restaurants and stores, and built and operated a methane-producing, organic waste digester that produces the equivalent of 15 percent of our system's electricity consumption. This reduced the amount of coal that needed to be burned to produce electricity, the amount of phosphorus in the lakes, and the amount of waste taken to the landfill. Dairy digesters are common in Europe but not in the United States. It is also uncommon for a health system to take a part of its savings, partner with a county, and build a system to improve the local environment and economy. It was easy to take the federal start-up grant, but it was a ton of discipline to make it work.

Leaders often talk about how hard it is to work with the government. In our perspective, "government" is not a single entity. There are thousands of parts of city, county, state, and federal governments. We treat these groups no differently from the way we treat other potential partners. If they share our values and focus on the greater good of the public, then we are happy to work with them.

When we noticed that methane produced by the degradation of waste from the county landfill was being burned off by open air flame, and the landfill was just one mile from one of our larger medical clinics, we saw an opportunity to partner with the county government. The county provided the pipeline for the methane, and we provided the electrical generation engine. The county and its taxpayers receive more than $200,000 in payment each year for the methane, which powers that entire campus, saving us money every day. The region wins financially, we keep our costs down, and fewer fossil fuels are burned. This is a great partnership with a like-minded local government. And the investment return was great. Staff was proud, the community was proud—these successes were adding up to easier recruiting across the system, attracting individuals with similar values. Many times I was stopped in a hallway of the clinic or hospital and a staff member would say, "I am very proud that our work is being recognized." Regardless of shifting state or federal priorities, we can take action locally. When you do so, your people will take pride in what you do.

We started down this energy path to lessen our negative impact on the health of our communities. Our success was so significant that I was invited to the White House as a "Champion for Change," and I was invited to represent Gundersen in the Blue Zone of the Paris Climate Conference. We were the only US healthcare provider given the opportunity to speak—not because of our hopes or dreams but because of what we had accomplished. Fortune 500 companies and many nations proudly announced goals to reduce greenhouse gas emissions by 30 percent by 2030 and by 50 percent by 2050. In eight years, we dropped our emissions by 90 percent, and we saved money and improved the local economy while doing it!

GHS FOSSIL FUEL EMISSIONS IMPROVEMENT

EMISSIONS[1,2,3,4,5] (LBS.)	2008	2016	% REDUCTION
Carbon Dioxide[1,3,4]	72,386,372	1,626,831	(98%)
Particulate Matter[1,5]	434,928	11,172	(97%)
Mercury[1,2]	2.39	0.16	(94%)

NOTE: The 2016 CO_2 value is the net sum after adjusting facility utility energy consumption with clean energy produced by GHS renewable energy projects.

SOURCES:
1 U.S. EPA AP-42
2 Practice Greenhealth's Energy Impact Calculator Data Sources: http://www.eichealth.org/calctest2.asp#
3 U.S. EPA eGRID Version 1.0 Year 2007 Summary Tables: http://www.epa.gov/egrid
4 U.S. EPA eGRID 10th edition Version 1.0 Year 2012 Summary Tables: http://www.eap.gov/egrid
5 Air pollution from electricity-generating large combustion plants (pdf), Copenhagen: European Environment Agency (EEA), 2008, ISBN 978-92-9167-355-1

*Numbers are projected with 11 of 12 months' consumption history in 2016.

This is an example of a disciplined disregard for conventional wisdom. We did not believe the oft-quoted choice between "jobs or the environment" or "the health of the economy or the environment." With courage and imagination, you can move beyond those binary choices.

NOTHING GOES *AWAY*—IT GOES SOMEWHERE

We improved the air quality, but what about that baby in the nursery we talked about? What about the one hundred chemicals in that baby's blood when it was born? Do we have any responsibility for those? Can we take on those responsibilities and not disrupt care or increase costs?

What happens to chemicals, antibiotics, cancer drugs, and hormones if they're dumped down a drain? First, who would do that, you ask? It turns out, almost everyone—individuals, hospitals, clinics, and manufacturers. There are fewer restrictions than most would think. But if they go through the sewage treatment system, doesn't that take care of the problem? No, not even close. Even well-functioning modern systems are not built to take out many of these helpful agents that turn into dangerous pollutants as they pass through the system and go into our water and soil. Once again, through being close to the work and asking deep enough questions, it became pretty clear that we are part of the problem. Few like to admit that because it puts pressure on them to do something about it.

Eric Bashaw is a chemist by training but a relentless detective by practice. He worked hard to convince us not to throw everything down the drain. He visited the sewage treatment facility many times to understand how it did and did not work. He also asked what was in the seventeen barrels of hazardous pharmaceutical waste that was leaving our loading dock every month. To find out, he dumped it all on a table and, along with our sustainability coordinator, Tom Thompson, dug through it. This was truly getting close to the work, and it was certainly taking a risk, but it was the only way to get to the core of the problem. Interesting things can be learned by digging through your everyday trash, but digging through your hazardous waste is especially enlightening.

Early on, we found hundred-milliliter bottles of medication—stacks of them—with only ten milliliters used out of every single one of them. We went to the nursing unit that disposed of the bottles and asked, "Why are you throwing these away?" They told us that for infection control reasons, you can enter the bottle only once. Once you have taken a dose out, you can't do it again, so you have to throw it away.

We then went to the person who ordered the medication and asked, "Hey, what's going on with this? They're throwing away all this medication." The man told us that the medication should be used, not thrown away. We told him that the nurses had explained to us that once the bottle had been entered once, the remaining medication had to be thrown away. He explained that he bought the medication in quantity because it was a bargain—it was so much less expensive that way. But, in fact, it was actually a terrible deal because most of it had to be thrown away. Furthermore, it was extremely expensive because the bottle, the water the medication was in, and the medication itself all had to be managed as hazardous waste.

The key to eliminating this source of hazardous waste was getting close to the work and taking the time to question why. It first required the commitment to do better for the community and then the discipline to go back upstream and find out why people were doing what they were doing.

We sat down and got the nursing staff and the buyer on the same page. If you buy only the more expensive 10-milliliter bottles, the nurses can empty the bottles. Thus, instead of having to put the bottle with the unused portion into hazardous pharmaceutical waste, the disposal of which is expensive, we can put the empty bottle in the regular recycling (which we get paid for).

Between what we made on the recycling and what we didn't have to pay for in hazardous pharmaceutical waste, we ended up saving thousands of dollars each month. We initially had a seventeen-fold drop in our hazardous waste. With ongoing efforts to change, study, measure, and change again, in six years our cost is down 93 percent and the volume of our hazardous pharmaceutical waste is twenty times less. These results are good for the environment and lower the cost of delivering care. This won't eliminate all the chemicals in the newborn baby's blood stream, but it is a good start on the ones for which we need to take responsibility.

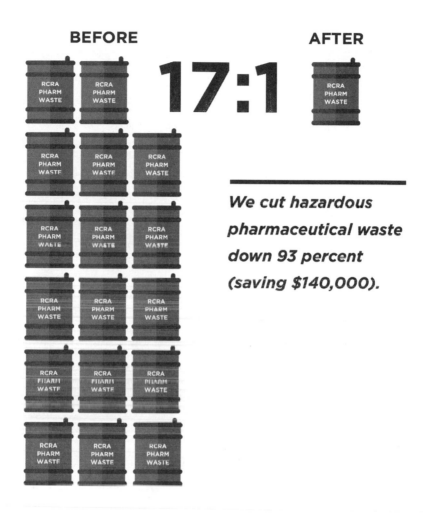

BEFORE

AFTER

17:1

We cut hazardous pharmaceutical waste down 93 percent (saving $140,000).

WHO IS LEADING?

The construction industry has not needed prodding to get involved when it comes to green initiatives. Consider this: The national CleanMed conference for healthcare providers draws seven hundred to one thousand attendees each year, but the Green Build meeting of construction industry leaders draws nearly twenty thousand! The response on our campus was no different.

At an internal construction management staff meeting it was asked how much of our renovation or new construction waste was being recycled? Were we filling up the landfills, or were we being more thoughtful? We didn't know. We decided that it would be consistent with everything else we did to ask the construction companies to reduce waste and recycle as much as possible.

This request led to arguments among our group. Some thought that it would be a terrible idea and that we would not get anyone to bid on the jobs if we asked them to meet a standard higher than others in the area demanded. Others felt that these were smart, adaptable, caring business owners and that they would find a way to decrease waste and keep the cost down. The latter won the day, and our material going to the landfill dropped to below 10 percent for renovation and to less than 5 percent for new construction. No added costs, just added value delivered by innovative builders who just needed to be challenged. They came through with great performance.

Another great performance, not from engineers or construction experts but from frontline staff, came out of the kitchen. Back in chapter 5, we talked about giving staff tools so they could contribute their insights, make changes, and feel like they could make a difference. One of the great tragedies in our country is the waste of an estimated 50 percent of all food products produced. With a small amount of training, we believed that our kitchen staff could make a meaningful dent in that problem. Dietary staff used an A3 to describe the current state and to measure, change, and then remeasure and plot their results. The process stimulated internal changes in ordering, processing, menu development, food preparation, and serving time. Over a period of several years, we reduced our food waste by over 90 percent and delivered thousands of meals each year to the Salvation

Army shelter. Our staff felt respected and proud of what they had accomplished.

Reducing food waste was another successful piece in the whole sustainability package. Many people thought we were completely misguided when they noticed we were going to take on this broad array of challenges. We certainly had to endure steady criticism along the way. What won the day was staying at it and maintaining focus on the big goals. Goals succeeded because they were backed by values that served the greater good, not a short-term, internally focused bonus system. The advantages for the organization went way beyond just decreasing our pollution, saving money, or improving the economy of the region. The staff was very proud of this work and their contribution to it.

Living our values to serve multiple needs in the community engaged our staff and helped with recruiting. We have had doctors, administrators, pharmacists, and nurses choose to work for us over other places because of our sustainability efforts. A local university chancellor said 30 percent of his students have sustainability as a core value—not an interest or a hobby but something they identify as a core tenet of their lives. They will use the behavior of their employer as a key yardstick for both where they will work and their connectedness to that work.

Were all our efforts great victories? It would be great if all our efforts had the 60 percent return that we had on conservation and the morale boost of hitting 100 percent power by renewables. But it turns out that the "bleeding edge" is called that for a reason. We had many struggles, too.

A BIG FAIL

It looked like it could be our greatest victory. We noticed that a brewery less than a mile away from our campus had a large building full of discarded mash that was slowly decomposing before it could be put into the sewer system. The mash was releasing a continuous stream of methane that was being burned off in two flames of Olympic torch proportions, all day, every day. The torches were burning what seemed like an endless supply of energy. After testing it, retesting it, and working out the details with the brewery, we set up a massive engine and started making electricity for the health system from beer gas!

The crowd went wild. All of our quality awards, breakthrough innovations, and national awards paled compared to the excitement around our new novel success. It was a great engineering and public relations success . . . at first. News of our cleverness and innovative thinking went viral. It showed up on more than ten thousand websites. It was on the large public screens in Los Angeles, New York City, and Las Vegas—people thought it was very cool that a hospital was making electricity out of brewery waste.

Soon, reality bit back. Just weeks after implementation, we noticed that the engine was being damaged by the gas. We found that the brewery had shifted from making beer to producing more hard lemonade-type products and were cleaning the containers with sulfuric acid, a compound deadly to engines.

A very pointed conversation then occurred. "Hey," we said, "how about if you stop doing that?" And they refused (they were selling tanker loads of this product). The industry norm is once you start selling a popular product, you don't change anything. Nothing in your recipe, handling, or cleaning changes. They simply were not going to alter anything that went into producing one of their bestsellers.

And so, despite expensive efforts to clean the gas, it kept destroying our engine, and eventually we had to move the engine to the dairy digester site.

It was a fail. And we lost money on it. We abandoned that project because although we could have taken the sulfur out, it would have been at an overall loss. Our egos were less important than the well-being of the organization. We had to admit the failure and move on.

There were some who thought that this setback was reason to abandon our energy initiatives. But we persisted. The key to finding the strength to carry on is going back to the mission to serve the community and our region. We looked not at individual successes or failures but at the program as a whole. We asked, were we being good stewards of the community's trust?

In chapter 10, we talked about using the gold in your basement. We were doing that. We were going to invest it in energy development projects in the community that would help the community's economy, decrease our dependence on fossil fuels, and save money for Gundersen.

True to form, our leaders and our board wanted to measure how our investments in environmental projects were doing against our more standard investments. The results were striking. Our organization's return from general funds for the organizations across a range of investments was 5 to 6 percent (2008–2015). Our returns from our environmental program as a whole were 10 to 12 percent. The mind-set shift was very important. We had to say, "What's the best use of these funds?" We didn't make a guess and use hope as a strategy. We worked very hard to prove that taking a portion of our investment portfolio and investing in our long-term regional infrastructure was good for the environment and good for our finances.

INVESTMENT RETURN 2008-2015

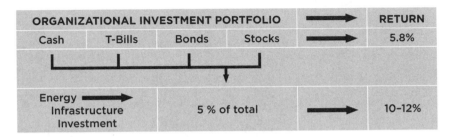

ORGANIZATIONAL INVESTMENT PORTFOLIO					RETURN
Cash	T-Bills	Bonds	Stocks		5.8%
Energy Infrastructure Investment		5 % of total			10-12%

(2014: Ceased Fossil Fuel Investment.)

Our purpose was to improve the health and well-being of the community. For us, that meant the whole community and all of its parts. Simply buying expensive green energy or pointing out to others their contribution to the toxins in our environment would not be enough. We had to have the courage to admit that we were part of the problem and then change how we lived and worked. Setting a goal to use only renewable energy is admirable. Setting goals to use only renewables in a way that decreases cost and improves the local economy is much more ambitious but doable. Having a board willing to take on the challenge of using our savings differently was a gift—many boards would not be this brave. Finally, taking on the responsibility to decrease our negative effects beyond our walls and to become a positive driving partner with the community was unusual, but it is becoming much more common.

Amazing things can happen when you have a values-driven board, values-driven leaders, and values-driven staff serving the community.

CHAPTER 11 TAKEAWAYS

☐ Set extraordinary goals to accomplish extraordinary achievements.

☐ Conventional wisdom is often an impediment to progress.

☐ You can improve the economy, the environment, and the bottom line at the same time.

☐ Measure and change; measure some more, and change some more.

☐ Take responsibility for your impact on your community.

☐ Build plans to accomplish multiple goals.

CHAPTER 12

LEAD ACROSS
THE DIVIDE

Create great strength with shared
values and a big tent.

Judy Kuipers had a great idea: bring the public university where she served as chancellor to the table with a private university with whom they competed as well as a two-year technical college that neither the public nor the private university had treated very well. Then, just to make it interesting, Kuipers invited two healthcare systems that openly aired each other's dirty laundry to join what would eventually become The La Crosse Medical Health Science Consortium. Each of these organizations had made efforts to address the short supply of nurses, physical therapists, physician assistants, dental assistants, and other healthcare workers, but, with minimal coordination, the results were nowhere near what the groups might accomplish together. The key question was what could they do together that individually was not possible? For starters, state money was available to build a facility, provided the community would commit to match the state funds. Philanthropic assistance was likely, but no single organization could guarantee matching funds on its own. However, together they could. As we learned in chapter 10, a facility is just a tool, but it can be a very important tool, a focal point, and a symbol that we care more about progress than about our own turf or egos.

The facility was built, education was expanded, and the partnership worked well. Competition gave way to selected collaborative success. But we were still far from our potential. Ten years after the Consortium's formation, the group decided to expand its mission from beyond the education it was providing to serving the community more broadly.

A consistent approach to diversity training and performance across the education, healthcare, and business communities was badly needed. Together, the five consortium partners developed a single diversity education curriculum. That way, regardless of which entity oriented you for a new job, you would receive the same diversity education. The module then spread beyond these organizations into other willing community businesses.

Likewise, we had three schools of nursing within the area. Scheduling the student nurses for their classes and clinical sites was a scramble. The overlap between educational and healthcare systems was a natural fit, but it was complex and messy. The group sat down together and worked through a combined scheduling system for both classroom and clinical activities so that the nursing students would have an adequate amount of time to prepare for both of those endeavors. This was more efficient for the students, the staff, and the organization.

Without the consortium's infrastructure and clear message that cooperation for the good of the community was an expected standard, both diversity education and scheduling for nursing students would have suffered.

There were many successes, but one of the biggest improvements was when we broke from tradition and broadened the tent even more. Historically, you could not hold a board seat in the consortium without being one of the founding, paying members. We changed that—to reach our potential we needed to expand our mission and our tent even more. We added a regional healthcare provider to broaden our perspective. Then, to help healthcare move outside its walls and to help the education community connect its students to the work of *health*care not just *sick* care, we invited the director of the county health department and the superintendent of schools to be board members. The expanded group established a population health committee to inspire and promote action. Among its many accomplishments, the committee drove a measurable decrease in binge drinking in young adults and reactivated the Community Coalition on Mental Health. Led by Brenda Rooney, the committee built one of the first comprehensive interactive health scorecards.[45] They also instituted a yearly Health Summit of community participants to coordinate efforts and get better quicker together. We had the same values and priorities, but we put up a bigger tent to make progress in community well-being.

---

45   "Healthy County Initiative—La Crosse County," www.lacrosseconsortium. org/uploads/content_files/files/Healthy%20County%20Dashboard%202014.pdf.

Common values and common goals can build coalitions of competitors.

A MORE DIFFICULT COMPETITOR: POVERTY

As with the consortium, broadening our opportunities was a theme at an IHI national meeting. Don Berwick called together a group of CEOs from innovative, successful healthcare organizations for a presentation by a young endocrinologist from New York City. She was thoughtful, brilliant, and clear about how she had gotten to where she was. The critical addition to her great talent and work ethic was a program in Harlem called *Gateway*, which had organized healthcare mentors for middle and high school kids. The mentors would spend time with these students to show them what success looked like. The endocrinologist pointed out that staggering dropout rates that had plagued the middle and high school prior to implementation of the Gateway program had given way to impressive graduation rates. Many of the students who had participated in the program pursued higher education, just as she had gone on to medical school to become a doctor. Boston had used the same program, with the same stunning results. Don challenged us to go back to our own communities and meet the universal need for inspiration and opportunity for kids who would otherwise not have that opportunity. He did not advise that we duplicate the Gateway program but that we learn from others, adapt to our local situations, and find good partners.

In our own community, we too had economically disadvantaged children who were dropping out of school at an alarming rate—many of them from our growing minority populations. I contacted the superintendent of schools and asked, "What can we do, how can we organize, and how can we put this together?" We knew that our intervention would not be identical to New York's or Boston's, but we felt that we could build a program focused on the health sciences—the Health Science Academy—that would inspire students and give them a pathway to succeed in work and in life.

These are the thoughts of superintendent Jerry Kember on this new partnership:

> Most leaders recognize the value of creating strong partnerships with other organizations and the people that lead them. However, for the School District of La Crosse, Wisconsin, building positive working relationships with community leaders and the organizations they serve has been the hallmark of its success.
>
> Resources for all businesses, both public and private, are significantly limited and for many it has reached a critical point. Diminishing resources have forced all of us to work not only differently and more efficiently but also more collaboratively. For those viewing this challenge creatively, it has brought about some unlikely partners. Why would a hospital want to create a formidable partnership with the local school district? Certainly, it would be a generous thing for the hospital to do in serving its community, but is there something more to it than that?
>
> I'll get back to that partnership story, but first we must acknowledge the basic elements that are required for a partnership to succeed. First and foremost, there must exist a high level of trust between the partners. That degree of trust only comes after time and experience with one another has allowed a strong and positive relationship to develop. There is no fast-track to building trust. It takes time to develop the kind of relationship that is both meaningful and productive.

A formidable partnership also requires that there be something in it for every member. Will everyone benefit in some way from joining in the collaboration? Are the results and rewards real for everyone involved? Unless the partnership is a win-win that can further each organization's mission and bring success to all, it's unlikely that the effort will last over time.

All parties need to feel truly "at the table" when it comes to decision making. Throughout the stages of planning and implementation, everyone's voice must be heard and valued. In a true partnership, an interdependence of purpose develops over time, clearly demonstrating that one cannot "make it happen" without the other.

While serving in a leadership capacity of a pK-12 public school system, we were able to combine the interests, talents, and resources of numerous local organizations to bring exceptional learning opportunities to students. One of our greatest successes has been with Gundersen Health System. Dr. Jeff Thompson, CEO of Gundersen, was seeking ways to increase the diversity of his staff so they may better represent the demographics of the people they serve. The school district was already experiencing greater ethnic diversity within its student population. After exploring possibilities in other parts of the country, it was discovered that a program in Boston was finding success increasing the number of minorities entering the medical field. We assembled a team of healthcare professionals and local education leaders to study Boston's program. Then, together, we designed an initiative to meet the needs of our students, our organizations, and the community. This new, creative, hands-on option for local high school juniors and seniors was soon created and aptly named the Health Science Academy (HSA).[46] Since its implementation, the Health Science Academy has served hundreds of high school students and helped them discover the expansive number of careers that exist within the field of healthcare. As with every successful partnership, a strong working relationship built on mutual trust and respect accompanied by shared decision making and benefits for all involved has made the Health Science Academy a success to this very day. Partnerships endure the test of time and continue to bring positive results only when all the elements described are sustained through deliberate planning and collaboration.

All communities, large or small, have a multitude of resources available that are often left underutilized. Connecting with the leaders of organizations and businesses in your community to discover the common purposes and goals that you share can make a significant difference to those you serve. In the School District of La Crosse, it has resulted in exceptional learning opportunities for students that has distinguished its educational program from all the rest.

The partnership between Gundersen and the school system then spread to the partners in the consortium and developed into such a strong program that now most school districts in the region are asking to get their students into this ever-expanding life experience/curriculum. It wouldn't have gotten started without the challenge from Don Berwick or without willing partners who said, "We can do this." None of us were going to make any more money,

---

46   "Health Science Academy," School District of LA Crosse, https://www.lacrosseschools.org/programs-services/career-choice-education/health-science-academy/

but we thought we could improve the fabric of the community if we took kids who were struggling with school or who were not sure what they wanted to do and gave them an opportunity to see a way forward. They could be mentored by successful people, not CEOs of giant industries but by staff who do important work that has an enormous impact.

The Health Science Academy continues to have a profound effect on students. Some find healthcare professions that appeal to them. Others discover that the field is not for them, which is great to find out as a junior in high school rather than as a junior in college.

Not long ago, one of them said, "I found exactly where I want to be."

I said, "Well, you got to see heart surgeries. You got to see knee surgeries. You got see bombs go off at Fort McCoy in mock trauma exercises. So, where do you want to be?"

The student had other things in mind. "Oh, I want to be as far away from that stuff as I can be. I want to be in the finance department. I want to be an accountant."

When I asked another young woman how she enjoyed it, she said she loved her time in the program. I recognized her name. "I know your name. Are you related to a woman by that same name who works at the hospital?" I asked.

"Oh, yeah," she said. "That's my aunt. I love my aunt."

I said, "Well, I know your aunt and she is a lovely person and does a great job. She works in environmental services on the cardiac floor. So, are you thinking that's what you're going to do, the kind of work that your aunt does?"

"Oh, no," she says. "I'm going to be a nurse practitioner."

"Why is that?" I asked.

"They do great stuff," she answered, "and they don't have to work as hard as the doctors." (I am pretty sure that is not always true). So, this young woman has her path figured out pretty clearly.

Another great collaboration was with the YMCA and its approach to struggling teenagers. Like the Health Science Academy, our investment was small in terms of people and dollars and had a phenomenal return. One of our social workers, Sarah Johnson, bravely said, "Let me take this challenge and see if I can do something." So we allowed her to devote half her time to working with disconnected, poorly supported teenagers. The health system and the YMCA took on a problem no one wanted to pay for, but everyone wanted *something* done.

There are no easy solutions, but there are low-cost ways to connect. Sarah helped develop a large basket of options to interest teens—music, food, art, and exercise—to try to connect, build, and inspire. She soon found that many of the young men coming to the teen center had no positive role models in their lives, so she went to a local university and found a young man willing to volunteer for "Men's Night." Men's Night isn't much more than a group of teenage boys sitting around and talking with "Mark," who was a nineteen-year-old college junior at the time the effort began. Attendance varies—sometimes only one teen shows up, sometimes fifteen. Mark has no agenda; he just lets the boys ask him questions about anything. Could be sports, could be school, could be family issues. Sometimes the topics are pretty deep and pretty chewy. The kids look forward to conversations with Mark. Although some may need more formal counseling, Mark provides the kids with thoughtful, caring insights. Even though he's now graduated from college, Mark still comes back and does Men's Night, which is a great example of breaking out of a traditional mold and asking, what is the need? You might be wondering whether Mark gets paid for his service. Not in dollars, but he does receive the pleasure of contributing to the well-being of the kids in the community.

Sarah was so successful with this and her other programs, which serve hundreds of kids each year, that when the YMCA built an addition onto their facility, Sarah and YMCA staff applied to have the ragged house that had been the teen center replaced with a really nice facility. It would have a better music room, better sitting area, better kitchen, better everything. It would draw in even more students. All this happened on the energy, insight, and durability of Sarah Johnson. Were there services before? Some, but without the willingness of Gundersen and Sarah's leadership to look beyond pure monetary returns on investment to what would do the most good for the community, the program never would have flourished as it has. Sarah had to have the courage to say, "We can do this," and the organization had to be willing to say, "Let's partner with the YMCA and see what we can do for the health and well-being of the community."

The keys in working on these multiple community partnerships are not much different from the key to hiring employees: It's important to have a values match.

The partners' cultures don't have to match exactly, but similar values and similar goals are essential. If you don't have similar values, working together is going to be a mess, and if you don't have the similar goals, you won't be heading in the same direction and the partnership will lose focus and disintegrate.

DISTANT BUT TRUE PARTNERS

We have already discussed how values-driven leadership can have an amazing impact beyond your own walls. We were seeing remarkable results within our own community, but with these successes came an even bigger opportunity to have an impact on the global community.

Once again, a challenge from Don Berwick at IHI brought into focus an issue that we had considered but had not yet acted on. He pointed out that many parts of the world, especially Africa, had maternal death rates much higher than those of the United States and other Western nations—not a few percentage points higher but *a hundred times higher!* And child death rates were twenty to fifty times higher. "Surely with all your innovation and skills, you can find a way to make a difference," Don said. His challenge didn't raise issues we weren't aware of, but it was very poignantly presented. We agreed that with all our assets of people, talent, technology, and financial strength, it was reasonable to believe that we could help.

Many organizations in business, faith communities, and healthcare have staff with experience in international projects. The question is how to make it consistent with our mission and serve a broader community without taking anything from our previous commitments. How can we lead with humility and make gains that would be self-sustaining and benefit all partners? We felt that the opportunity to broaden our definition of "the communities we serve" was a reasonable first step. The opportunity for our staff to broaden their worldview, learn about resiliency and diversity, and raise their appreciation for other cultures was of great value to our staff-building plans.

To accompany that step, and being aware that ultimately health-care budgets are paid for by taxes, businesses, and individuals, our plan was to build these connections through local partnerships, philanthropy, and volunteers. Our goal was not to work in places where we could make money (many Western healthcare organizations were already on that path), or to take the cost of these activities unwillingly out of our local communities. We believed that we would find hundreds of volunteers, partners, and donors to help support the effort. We found all that and more.

We believed that these partnerships would improve the fabric of communities they touched, as well as the fabric of our staff. We called it *Global Partners*. Much of the experience our staff had been a part of in the past was with very important programs that do great work and address acute problems—trips to do surgeries or examinations once or twice a year. We believed that this was important work and that it should continue, but we also felt that there was an opportunity to develop an ongoing relationship with the broader community at home and in our partner sites. This isn't a mayor's meeting to talk economic development, this is frontline staff from many parts of each community working on plans for a shared goal: help get the community to the point where it no longer needs us. We wouldn't just do clinical health. We would work on housing, education, food sufficiency, water supply, and improving the ability and services of the local medical community.

We chose three areas outside of our region. One was in the highlands of Nicaragua, which is the second poorest country in our hemisphere. Nicaragua has lovely people but lacks adequate resources and infrastructure to provide medical care and education, especially in rural areas. Ethiopia also has enormous need—there's only one provider, on average, per thirty thousand (1:30,000) people—and we found local and regional partners with whom to combine our strengths. However, there was still plenty of need in the United States. We chose to work with the Peoples of the Pine Ridge and

Rosebud Reservations in South Dakota, who, as a group, may have the worst health in the country.

INTENTIONS ARE NICE, BUT IT'S THE OUTCOMES THAT MATTER

As a leader, when expending these types of resources outside your own area, you will always be challenged by the argument that there are many people in need closer to home. They are right. We try to do many things with our regional partners for them, as well. Our belief is we have a greater capacity than most imagine. We recognize that different people will be inspired by different needs and causes. We will do our best when we can tap into this very large reservoir of talent and caring. Our job as leaders is to inspire them with our courage to make a plan in the face of the critics, have the discipline to follow through on that plan, and then the immense durability to get through the endless bumps along this road. Tough? Yes. Worth it? Absolutely.

You might ask whom we would ever get to take on three nations thousands of miles apart with no budget except what could be raised and with help coming entirely from volunteers across the community. We would get Liz Arnold. She is smart, hard-working, a great planner and builder, and, most importantly, a firmly values-based leader.

Liz has a full-time salary from Gundersen, but the money to keep the program going is all raised through a variety of fundraisers and donations. Travel, lodging, and meals are all at the volunteers' cost. Even the rebuilt village of Santa Celia mentioned below was donated one house at a time, or even parts of a house at a time, not from the organization but from individuals. Most valuable was that people volunteered their time. People took time off from their jobs in areas such as nursing, medical staff, respiratory therapy, biomedical engineering, and others to volunteer their efforts to work on these long-term plans. But nearly half of all participants come from the community-at-large. Universities, schools, civic organizations, and members of the faith communities have all contributed. Even the grade schools get involved, connecting to school children they probably will never meet in person.

We didn't choose Nicaragua because it was wealthy or could ever give us a financial return. We chose it because the area is remarkably underserved. We tried to lead humbly and to develop relationships with local groups. We did that with a hospital, clinics, and community improvement groups. Our volunteers travel there several times a year for extended periods to work with groups to teach nursing students and medical staff or to work in the schools or clinics.

The very rural village of Santa Celia sits atop a ridge next to a coffee plantation that provides what little employment is available. Village residents lived in one-room homes. They had no clean water, and what water they did have was brought by children, usually little girls, who spent much of the day walking down the mountain to get water instead of going to school. When I visited a local high school (there were no public high schools, only schools for scholarship-based students), I asked about the water supply. A quick hand went up and a very bright, articulate young woman pointed out there are four ways to get clean water: you can boil the water, you can put sanitizing pills in the water, you can use a water filter (although no one there had ever seen one), or you can place the water in two-liter soda bottles, put them on the roof, and after twenty-four hours in the sunlight, it will be pure (this is the method used most often).

The air is no better. Cooking was done in the middle of the one-room homes, which increased the prevalence of asthma and respiratory diseases in infants and children.

Although our and other's surgical outreach to developing countries provides tremendous advantages and changes lives for the better, simple public health measures in the interest of clean water and clean air also have great potential. We worked with our Rotary Club partners (one of the great service groups in the world) and obtained water filters for each of the homes in the community. With less need to spend all day carrying water, it became more likely that the young girls would stay in school, which is critical to the economic health of the community.[47]

Although education on water and air problems was done, ultimately building new housing units with concrete floors, solid walls, windows, and a small but effective outside cooking space markedly decreased respiratory illnesses in the village.

Confirming what public health experts and statisticians have known for a long time, a grandmother pointed to the cleaner water and better air and said that it "helps the babies live, so now the young moms don't have to have so many babies." This is one of the holy grails of public health that is so often overlooked. The impact of cleaner water and air on the long-term health, strength of the community, and the opportunities for the young women and men has been immeasurable.

The health of women in any culture is an important identifier of community health. Mindful of that, in addition to our other community and hospital efforts, we worked with the local Fara clinic and other organizations to expand and improve cervical and breast

---

47   Shannon Murphy, Wivinia Belmonte, and Jane Nelson, "Investing in Girls' Education," Harvard Kennedy School, September 2009, www.hks.harvard.edu/m-rcbg/CSRI/publications/report_40_investing_in_girls.pdf.

cancer screening by training local health workers, radiologists, and surgeons.[48]

We hope to teach and learn. Volunteer teams have trained more than two hundred midwives and community health workers in skills to resuscitate a baby at birth, established five lending libraries, led workshops for more than five hundred teachers and secondary students on how to teach math and reading to primary students and more.

We try to measure. We try to show progress. However, this is not all altruism. There's an advantage to having people from our community witness the courage and durability of people in under-resourced areas and then come home and be reminded of what they have. They tend to be more thoughtful, waste less, complain less, and are generally more grateful.

Our goal was to connect to international sites to help build ourselves along with them. Our goals have not been to do things for them but to work *with* them so that in five, fifteen, or twenty-five years, they no longer need our help. We would then be free to do this work in other areas. A final goal, as noted before, was to have a residual effect on our staff and our community that would enhance their understanding of different cultures, enhance gratefulness, and build both teams and individuals. Here's what one participant, Renee, had to say in an email exchange with her staff about the experience and the effect on her and those in her department:

> I recently shared my Nicaragua trip at a staff meeting. As you know, I was a bit nervous volunteering this year as I have a

---

48   Ana Revenga and Sudhir Shetty, "Empowering Women is Smart Economics," *Finance & Development* 49, no. 1, www.imf.org/external/pubs/ft/fandd/2012/03/revenga.htm.

new role as clinical manager. My staff did a fantastic job in my absence, but I felt that it would be a great opportunity to share with them my experiences and exactly what their clinical manager was doing on this trip. The PowerPoint does not completely tell the story, but I shared with them my great experiences guided by the pictures in the presentation. It was moving, as their clinical manager, to share this with my staff. In fact, here is a response I received from one of my staff members. I am very happy that I presented, as I feel that I have also moved several of my staff members regarding the focus of these trips. Enjoy!

And I would like to thank you for all you and the Global Partners staff do to facilitate these trips. You all do an amazing job and I cannot thank you enough!

"Renee,

I am so glad you enjoyed your trip and you made it back safe and sound. I wanted to let you know that your commitment and dedication to improve the lives of others from other cultures so far away is impressive in an almost indefinable way and shows incredible leadership! I was really moved by your talk today and view you as a true hero. I got goose bumps and felt my eyes getting watery as you told your story. Your passion and love for the people of Nicaragua and the lives you were able to touch there was beaming. I could also see the solidarity bond which grew between you and your cohorts and that is a powerful thing, as well. I know your presentation was just the tip of the iceberg of your experience and maybe someday you could share more about it with me. I have always wanted to be part of an experience like yours because of a yearning to make a difference in our world. What an opportunity of a lifetime that surely has changed you forever! Thank you so much for sharing with us!"

THE GIFT OF SERVICE

Early on, I discussed the ripple effect that leaders can have on those they lead. Good or bad, our choices have an influence well beyond our immediate environment. Great partnerships also have a positive effect well beyond those they first touch.

There are books upon books about the struggles and opportunities in Africa, a huge and diverse continent with some of the most asset-rich and asset-poor places on the planet. Our work in Ethiopia has barely begun. Yetabon is a few hours south of Addis Ababa. It is rural, poor, and outside the focus of most groups. There we have partnered with local groups and with a group called Project Mercy. In Ethiopia, we have not yet seen great victories of the sort we witnessed in Nicaragua, and there have been no substantial changes in the long-term health of the community. But we are there. We have already changed many lives with vision screening and treatment of trachoma for the twelve hundred children at the PM school, establishing "teach and treat" models of care in podiatry and dental work, as well as teaching the Helping Babies Breathe curriculum to hospital staff and midwifery students.

Dr. Mike Jacobs is a great clinician. He has served as a department chair, an elected board member, and at this time is currently one of Gundersen's four medical vice presidents. He has performed many surgeries and has taught other local doctors to perform them, as well. But he also spent time in Ethiopia helping to wash feet and fit shoes on a population that depends largely on shoeless feet as their mode of transportation. The following is an excerpt of a message that Mike posted on the Global Partners blog site.[49]

---

49 "Ethiopia," Gundersen Health System, www.gundersenhealth.org/
our-system/global-partners/ethiopia/.

Some members tied up loose ends at the hospital this morning after several days of surgery while the rest of us spent our last day with a focus on TOMS shoes. 675 pair dispensed, with every foot washed. Well done, Team!

I noticed a man working in the soil around my [cottage]. He had been turning the soil with a one-hand tool. This continued on and off during our stay. I approached and greeted him. I could see the years of physical labor on his face. What was more pronounced was his joy. This was visible in his eyes and smile. His work is typical of Ethiopians, yet passion and love is expressed daily. This man represents a joy that is void of material wealth. Project Mercy would tell you, it is not the hospital, it is not the school (serves 1,500 students), it is not the home for children, it is not the water program, and it is not the farming project. Project Mercy would tell you the reason for his joy would be God's presence, mercy, and grace. You may agree, or disagree, however I have witnessed Project Mercy in action. It is all true. Global Partners, Project Mercy, and Ethiopia continue to make joyful partners.

Our contributions will be lasting for the Ethiopians, but their gift to our staff and to those whom our staff touches will be equally enduring.

The final place we chose to partner with may have the worst health in the United States: The Pine Ridge and Rosebud Indian Reservations of South Dakota. Life expectancy on the reservations is twenty-five to thirty years shorter than most other parts of the country. They are a great people who face tremendous challenges in housing, employment, education, addiction, and mental health.

After a stunning visit to Wounded Knee, I asked Edgar Bear Running what we could work on together—what could both the native peoples and the many volunteers across our region do together that would have a lasting impact? The 60–80 percent unemployment rate was too daunting an issue from which to begin. Smoking cessation efforts in this region, which had an adult smoking rate estimated to be "almost everyone," was also foreboding but held possibilities. However, screening for breast cancer could be improved easily because almost all the women needed it.

Adding to the density of problems was a complex history of relationships between the tribes, the Bureau of Indian Affairs, the state, and many other agencies. Daunting indeed, but as we have seen throughout this book, daunting is no excuse to go weak on your values. It didn't take much courage to work with this group. Most are lovely people with big hearts and great resilience. But it did take durability to stay with a plan and tolerate the many roadblocks, adapt to the changing dynamics, and coordinate all the pieces to move forward.

POINTS OF LIGHT IN THE DARKNESS

Similar efforts are yielding positive results with our native partners, where we have worked to develop a deep level of trust with the community. Breast screening is underway, and in less than six years we have increased the percentage of eligible women receiving mammograms from 9 percent to 43 percent. Many children and adults are getting examinations that help them to get earlier care. But the benefits to those we partner with have been matched by the personal enrichment in those of us who have engaged in these efforts and then returned to our own communities. We are also beginning to offer more medical education talks and trainings to our IHS partners. And we've recently added behavioral health consultative support for the clinic.

Partners across our community, such as the school system, churches, universities, and healthcare volunteers, made these gains possible; however, there was one partnership we did not anticipate: The Health Science Academy (HSA). This is the group we mentioned earlier—junior and senior high school students who commit half of their education time to doing more field work, hands-on experiences, and being mentored in the healthcare sector. Their innovative leaders extended their activities to participation in our programs—to work with the people, especially adolescents, living on the reservations.

At the end of the year, HSA students design and present posters that reflect the most significant things that happened in that year. They include photographs of themselves going to heart surgeries, knee replacements, mock trauma exercises, or studying anatomy with cadavers. Kids who went with our Global Partners staff to South Dakota often made that experience their poster's centerpiece. Heart surgeries, knee surgeries, and all the other things they've seen pale in comparison to getting in a van and spending a week with kids on the reservations.

It's no wonder that the Global Partners' trips to the reservations profoundly affects HSA students: new culture and new challenges, and exposure to enormous social issues, as evidenced by a thirty-two-mile event called The Suicide Awareness Walk/Run/Bike. Every few miles along the route, there's a water and refreshment stand at which a family has created a display for their child, relative, or loved one who succumbed to suicide. The thirty-two-mile walk seems pretty minor compared with the journey those families have been on.

Another example are the leadership camps where the HSA kids can sit down with the native kids their age and talk about serious issues concerning families and the struggles of living with such high rates of unemployment, alcoholism, diabetes, and traumatic injuries. It is always slow at first but trust builds, friendships are formed, and much deeper learning and understanding is made possible.

HSA graduate Hayden Jobe traveled twice with HSA and Global Partners to Pine Ridge. He taught a youth leadership camp, took part in organizing health fairs, and even demonstrated first aid techniques.

"It changed my life in ways I couldn't have experienced anywhere else," says Hayden. "It gave me a much better understanding of the Lakota people and culture. It made me realize how lucky I am for what I have and grateful for the opportunities that I have to learn.

"Through all of these experiences I have learned that it is very important to help communities in need, but also you can take what you learn from them and apply it to your own community and help people wherever you are."

This will change his worldview at home, school, work, and in his community. It may be hard to measure the return on investment but, clearly, community building starts with one young leader at a time.

Finally, on another poster, a young woman from HSA also had many pictures about Pine Ridge—friends she had made, groups she had been a part of, and projects she had worked on. It dominated her year. But she had one other unique piece. In the exact middle of her poster, for her centerpiece, she had an open space with a hand-written note. It read: "I've never before volunteered for anything in my life, and after going to work a week at Pine Ridge, I will be a lifelong active volunteer."

When I asked her about it her eyes welled up and she said that when she first went to the reservation, she was very unsure about what she could do and how to interact. She now felt she had a great deal to offer to Pine Ridge and was very interested and willing to reach out and connect in other settings for the rest of her life! It's hard to put a number on that, but it truly is invaluable to the long-term health and well-being of any community lucky enough to have her.

Our goal was to find partners with the same values and similar goals. We worked with as broad a tent as possible to gather more talent and more insight. It was not hard to find people and organizations of similar mind sets willing to work for something bigger than themselves. Leading humbly, learning in both directions, and looking for both short-term and long-term wins provides adequate guidance to get started in your listening to become a great partner. The service we provide is significant and noble. The return is immeasurable.

CHAPTER 12 TAKEAWAYS

- ☐ Communities have huge untapped capacity; our job is to inspire and unleash it.
- ☐ Cast a broad tent to find partners with similar values.
- ☐ Partnerships with common values and agreed-upon goals will be much more efficient.
- ☐ Learning will go both ways, and benefit will go both ways.
- ☐ These partnerships can have an impact on your staff that will serve you and your community far beyond their immediate involvement.

CONCLUSION

WHEN VALUES LEAD, WE ALL WIN.

Jumping off a train

We were coming back from an international Boy Scout Jamboree in Idaho on a chartered train. The train stopped for fuel about twenty miles from my hometown. But they weren't going to let any of us off; we were all going to have to get off hours away near Chicago. So, to save my parents that ten-hour round-trip, I convinced another teenager from my area to jump off the train with me. Only, when the train stopped, our train car was on a bridge more than a hundred feet over the water. There was no way we could jump off while the train was stopped.

We changed plans and decided to jump from the train as it passed the station platform. By the time we reached the platform, the train was moving rather quickly. The kid I was with got scared.

"It's going to be a long walk from Chicago!" I told him, leaping from the train with a laugh.

I hit the platform in a tumble of arms and legs, my backpack and souvenirs scattering about. I got up and dusted myself off just as he jumped off. He hit the platform and rolled around in the same hilarious fashion. We were both fine—everything had worked out. That is, except for the rather massive tongue-lashing we both received from the stationmaster, who went ballistic that we had jumped off a fast-moving train onto his platform. My mother was also not amused, but my dad thought it was great—saved him ten hours of driving.

Of course, a kid making a plan, finding the courage to implement it, and having the durability to take a rocky landing to lessen the burden on his parents is not the same as the struggles that affect countless lives, which we've detailed in this book. But it is symbolic of the decisions we will have to face in each of our lives. Do we have the courage to make the leap—to act on what we value? Can we find the discipline to stay with it and are we durable enough to persist despite difficulty and criticism?

Remember our ripple from the introduction? We talked about how individual actions can create ripple effects of change. The stories shared in this book exemplify how powerful of an impact people can have when they lead with their values.

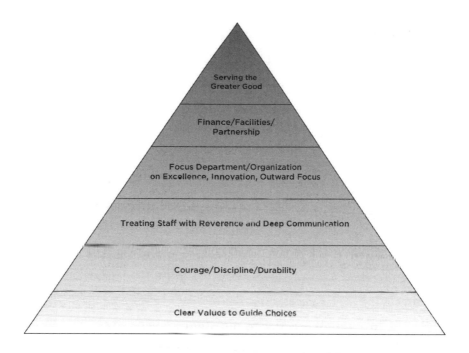

While the affects you can have on others and the community as a whole can be seen as a ripple, a pyramid is a perfect example for understanding how this progresses. You start with your core values that guide your choices—this is your foundation. We discussed how courage, discipline, and durability are the core pillars of values-driven leadership. These pillars are what support the larger structure of a values-based culture. Treating your staff with reverence and deeply communicating with them will ensure they are engaged, mindful, and compassionate. Once you have your values, your core support pillars, and an engaged staff, then you can focus your department or organization on excellence, innovation, and outward focus. At that point, you are ready to start using the gold in your basement to build new facilities or expand services that will serve the greater community. This opens the door to partnerships and coalitions aimed at serving the greater good.

Should you take the whole of these stories and strategies and try to implement them in your department, school, or organization, you will indeed be taking a leap. It may look easy on the page, but excellence isn't easy and doesn't follow a formula. It takes clarity of direction coupled with the talents and hearts of many to adjust and push beyond the norm. If you do leap, you might have to take a painful landing, but just like me leaping from that train, you'll find yourself a lot closer to where you want to be.

One of the plusses of courageous, disciplined, durable leadership is that it can inspire and touch the lives of countless individuals. Consider the ripple from the introduction; what kind of impact do you want to have? This is about something bigger than any of us. It requires a lot of hard work and dedication. Will you take this leap with me, in creating a better tomorrow for everyone? Will you let your values—not profits or personal gains—be your compass?

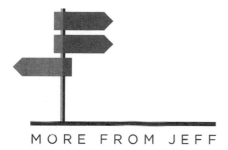

QUOTES FROM JEFF

- No one's ego is more important than the well-being of the patients or the staff.

- What you tolerate, you support.

- Innovation Keys:

  □ Get close enough to the work to feel the moral imperative.

  □ Use structure to improve innovation.

  □ Maintain a disciplined disregard for conventional wisdom.

- The more special and protected we treat the executives, the less special and more afraid the staff feel.

- "Holding accountable" is looking backward. "Being responsible for their success" is looking forward. Excellence will be found in the balance.

- The chain of command is always a weak link in the communication chain.

- Humble listening builds strong bonds to deeper values.

- Small-market competition is best replaced by disciplined, values-driven systems that commit to transparent, measurable improvements in the community's well-being.

- Without discipline, courageous decisions will do little good, because they'll go nowhere. Discipline gives courage legs.

- The ripple effect of undermanaged poor performance of leaders is enormous.

- There is often a big gap between doing something and accomplishing something.

- Collaboration will multiply your investment faster than the stock market.

- We need to move past the notion of excellence on the basis of reputation, marketing budgets, or size, and expect greatness to be described by broad outcome measures across time, demographics, and sectors of the community.

- Coalitions of competitors can find common values and common goals.

- The cultures of the partners don't have to match exactly, but you have to have similar values and similar goals. If you don't have similar values, then working together is going to be a mess, and if you don't have the same goals, then you won't be heading in the same direction, and the partnership will lose focus and disintegrate.

- We had to ignore the conventional wisdom of the day, which says a choice must be made either between jobs and the environment or between cost savings and the environment.

- Using silence to distance yourself from a critical situation is still a statement and an action. Silence is still a choice—one made in fear.

- Durability is needed to live your values outside the spotlight despite crisis and hardship.

- The balance is to celebrate your staff's successes without developing hubris or complacency.

- A strong organization with a steadfast commitment to its values will attract partners willing to make long-term investments.

- The more complicated the lives of our staff, the more they need us to understand those struggles.

- If you don't have the courage to implement your values, they are just words.

- Comparing yourself to your mediocre past or mediocre peers is not excellence.

- People won't remember your margins or your awards; they will remember how you treated them.

- Chaos and confusion—what a perfect place to start. This was an area where we could do the most good for those in the most need.

MORE ABOUT DR. THOMPSON'S WORK WITH CLIENTS

Dr. Thompson works with a broad range of clients as coach, advisor, or keynote speaker on the importance and power of values-based leadership. Through his work, he paints a realistic picture of what it takes to be a values-based leader and shows how this path shapes and supports a culture that benefits its people, the organization, and the broader community while delivering exceptional and sustainable results.

Dr. Thompson bases his work and keynotes on real-life stories pulled from across industries and sectors and identifies the key lessons leaders at all levels can apply to ensure they make the choices that propel the shared mission of the organization.

He offers his clients and audiences the understanding that values-based leadership is not just a noble idea but one that actually works, equips them with a framework with which to evaluate their own decisions as contributors and leaders, and inspires them to drive broad-based, meaningful change.

To learn more about advisory, coaching, or keynote opportunities with Dr. Thompson, visit him at
JeffThompsonMD.com